# Conversations about Heaven

# Conversations about Heaven

Difficult Questions about Our Eternal Home

## Brian G. Chilton

*Foreword by Leo Percer*

*Preface by Thomas J. Gentry II*

RESOURCE *Publications* · Eugene, Oregon

CONVERSATIONS ABOUT HEAVEN
Difficult Questions about Our Eternal Home

Resource Publications
An Imprint of Wipf and Stock Publishers
199 W. 8th Ave., Suite 3
Eugene, OR 97401

www.wipfandstock.com

PAPERBACK ISBN: 978-1-6667-6268-6
HARDCOVER ISBN: 978-1-6667-6269-3
EBOOK ISBN: 978-1-6667-6270-9

04/04/23

Unless otherwise noted, all Scripture quotations are taken from the Christian Standard Bible®, Copyright © 2020 by Holman Bible Publishers. Christian Standard Bible® and CSB® is a federally registered trademark of Holman Bible Publishers.

This book is dedicated to Sandy Riddle (pictured below), a lady who asked some of the most challenging questions about heaven that I have ever received. This book is also dedicated to the good folks at Huntsville Baptist Church in Yadkinville, North Carolina where I had the honor to serve as their pastor for numerous years. It was there that I delivered the messages and had the conversations with Sandy that served as the basis for this book's material.

Additionally, I would like to thank my family for their loving support (wife: Jennifer, son: Grayson). Finally, I would also like to thank Michelle Johnson and Dr. T. J. Gentry for their help in editing this book.

Sandy Riddle (1943–2019)

# CONTENTS

# FOREWORD

A S A SEMINARY PROFESSOR, questions and conversations are part of my daily experience. While such conversations may vary on topic, one constant comes up regularly—heaven. The questions may vary, but the focus remains the same. People want to know what they can about heaven. In one conversation, students waxed eloquent on what they considered our experience of heaven would be. The consensus was simple: Heaven would be a wonderful worship service in which people would enjoy singing songs to and about God forever. One student even noted, "Think of how great the band in heaven will be!" But then I had an awful thought—how long would I be able to endure a heaven where singing was the primary focus? Would I get bored? As I drove home that evening, I found myself a bit anxious. "How could I think of heaven as boring?" I couldn't shake the idea of constant singing being something that would ultimately cause me to lose interest. Then a verse from Paul came to my mind: "What no eye has seen, no ear has heard, and no human heart has conceived—God has prepared these things for those who love him." (1 Corinthians 2:9 CSB) I couldn't shake the words "what no human heart has conceived . . ." I began to realize that God's preparations for his people were in many ways beyond our comprehension, perhaps even beyond our wildest dreams. My anxiety slipped away as I realized that no ONE scenario could adequately depict the wonder of heaven in the presence of God. What a relief!

Questions about heaven vary, and the issues addressed in this book represent a sample of such questions from a variety of people. In this volume, Brian Chilton offers you his response to many questions he received from the people he served as pastor and from others. He states his intention clearly; he defines his approach well; he offers a cogent overview of the issues considered; and he supports his conclusions with solid research and passionate conviction. I think you will find yourself better equipped to deal with questions that may arise in discussions regarding heaven and related topics. This book addresses the topic of heaven and offers advice from Scripture and from sound reason as to how we may think about the issue. The material here offers the reader a wealth of information to answer difficult questions and to foster ongoing and deep conversation. Questions range from the location of heaven to the nature of resurrected bodies. You will even find some discussion on issues related to pets in heaven and the role of marriage in the afterlife. My favorite chapter is: Will heaven be boring? While I am sure that the answer is negative, I am even more sure that the reading of this book will provide helpful information for further discussions about heaven and God's eternal plan for humanity.

Brian Chilton was my student, most recently completing his Ph.D. in Theology and Apologetics at Liberty University. During his studies, we enjoyed many conversations and entertained many questions on a variety of academic and pastoral issues. These talks were deep and encouraging. When he told me about his sermon series on heaven (and later this book on the same subject), I admit that I looked forward to reading it. Brian is a good scholar and a fine preacher. I do not doubt that the journey upon which you are about to embark will not only be informative but will also be enjoyable and edifying. Since I had the honor of working on his dissertation team, I can assure you that this book will be well-researched and well-written.

I am honored to introduce this book to you. You will find here good advice from Scripture and from many good Christian resources. This topic is important both on an academic and pastoral level, and Brian Chilton is the right person (an academic and a pastor) to engage and encourage the conversation. I know the journey upon which you are about to embark, and I am sure that you will find the material here interesting, thought-provoking, and helpful. While familiar with some of the materials included here, I still envy those of you who will read this for the first time. The adventure will be worth the effort!

**—Leo Percer, PhD**
John W. Rawlings Associate Professor in Biblical Studies
Rawlings School of Divinity, Liberty University

# PREFACE

ERHAPS YOU FIND THE topic of heaven a mixture of hopefulness and mystery. The thought of the biblical picture of an eternal embrace by the perfect love of the Savior is compelling and ignites the heart and mind with visions of delight and joy, while the mystery of the reality of heaven leaves you with uncertainty based on not yet knowing. Take heart, friend. In the pages that follow, Dr. Brian Chilton writes with a pastor's heart and a scholar's mind as he introduces the topic of heaven in a conversational and engaging manner.

Perhaps the most delightful aspect of what awaits you is the kindness and warmth in the words and the sheer profundity of the message. I suspect that I will often return to these pages as a resource in my pastoral ministry and a balm for my heart that senses this world is not my final home. Heaven awaits the Christian in the future, but a glimpse of heaven—more than a glimpse—is here now, in Brian's work, for the serious and thoughtful reader. Enjoy these conversations about heaven. I dare you to hope for what is described in these pages.

—Thomas J. Gentry II

# INTRODUCTION

H AVE YOU EVER LOOKED around at the beauty of creation and marveled at how great a place this is? I have always loved astronomy, looking at the beautiful scenery of the universe. My wife gave me a telescope for Christmas one year. Even though it was freezing outside, I didn't care. I wanted to see the beauty of the stars and planets around our beautiful planet. When I looked at Jupiter through the powerful lens of the telescope, I was in awe. I could see the large red storm that had been shown on many television programs. Jupiter's numerous moons seemed to dance with light as they encircled the massive planet. Then, I turned my attention to Saturn. Its rings were phenomenally crisp and clear in the telescope's sight. It was as if I could reach up to clasp the rings as one would take a frisbee. But that was not the truly epic moment of the night. The main event, so to speak, was when I positioned the telescope in the direction of the Andromeda Galaxy. I was amazed to see this distant galaxy. From my perspective, it looked like a blue, hazy, egg yolk. What an amazing thing to consider! This nearby galaxy which is 2.537 million light-years away was visible to me. I felt incredibly small at the moment—which isn't exceedingly difficult being that I am a mere 5' 7" tall. I tell everyone that I used to be 5' 8", but the doctor told me that I had shrunk an inch. I guess that can be attributed to all my years of weightlifting. Well, that's the more macho theory. More likely, it stems from my genetic predisposition to being vertically challenged.

Despite the grandeur of creation, we easily understand that something is wrong with the universe. The universe itself is finite. The universe as we know it is expanding at the rate of 44.74 miles per second or 72 kilometers a second. The expansion rate is speeding up as time moves along, meaning that by the time you read this statement, the universe is expanding faster than it was when I first penned it. Some have postulated that the universe will eventually reach a point where life will no longer be able to exist.

Not only does the evidence suggest that life will not remain in this universe forever, but an observer will quickly detect the depravity in human nature. Some may think this is a horrid view to take, leading to a pessimistic outlook. Instead, such a view is supported by the numerous cases of crime and warfare that have occurred over time. When people are left to themselves, many choose to destroy rather than help another person in need.

All of this suggests that something better must exist. One may dream of an eternal land where death and decay do not exist—a land of beauty and perfection, and one of peace and harmony. I mean, ask anyone on the Miss America circuit, and the contestants will tell you that they desire world peace. Part of this yearning comes from an innate desire to call some place our permanent, eternal home.

## The Importance of Home

Having a place to call home is important to a person. My first experience of homesickness occurred when I left home for Hendersonville, North Carolina to attend Fruitland Baptist Bible College. The first few days were horrible! I missed my family. I longed to see my parents and my sister. This was before I was married. Even still, I realized during this experience how bad homesickness can be. A few years later, my sister called me in tears when she first began her academic career at East Carolina University due to her experience of homesickness. I could relate because of suffering from the homesick blues.

My second experience of homesickness was not as intense as the first. In full disclosure, I am a person who desires and requires privacy and solitude at certain times. For those who care to know, I tested as an INTJ on the Myers-Briggs personality test. The introverts reading this will quickly identify with our need to have alone time to recharge and recuperate from all the social interactions we are forced to attend.

When my family and I lived in the small town of Yadkinville, North Carolina, we didn't have much privacy. Our home was in a nice, friendly neighborhood just off a major highway. Our neighbors were wonderful! They were kind, compassionate people. However, even while at my house, I never truly felt at home because I could not get the peace and solitude that I needed.

I often felt homesick because I couldn't seem to find the time or space needed to spend alone with God. A landscaping business was positioned behind our house, and a print shop was to the side of us. Next to the print shop was a rental house. Across the street sat an auto parts store with homes arranged down the street beside it. Homes were aligned to the side of our house down our side of the street. There was no privacy. No privacy at all.

My wife, Jennifer, knew that this bothered me. She did everything in her power to combat the problem. We built a fence that surrounded a prayer garden that we had created. The prayer garden featured a firepit and an area to get some semblance of solitude. The prayer garden helped tremendously, but even the prayer garden did not always provide the peace and solitude that I needed. Once while sitting in my prayer garden, I was reading a book—something that my bibliophile friends will appreciate—when I looked up from my theological book only to find some customer at the landscaping business staring at me. He looked dumbfounded to see a person reading a book. Could it have been that he was amazed that someone wasn't on their tablet or phone? Or was he so enamored by the possibility that someone might like to read the printed page that he lost all his couth? Whatever the reason, the man did not give me just a brief gaze. He gave me a long deep stare—one that caused an uncomfortable feeling of unrest. Not many people can find rest while knowing that someone is staring them down. At least, I cannot. I threw up my hands with the book in hand and went back inside my home.

We later moved to Westfield, North Carolina. There, we lived in a parsonage. Even though our location changed, the feelings of homesickness did not subside. I was constantly reminded that the parsonage was not my home; not by the people of the church, per se, but more from the cognitive remembrance that we were not able to do certain things that we could in our own house. For instance, we were not able to plant a tree or a bush where we wished because we couldn't take it with us when we left. To make matters worse, a constant carousel of individuals parked in the church parking lot and shined their headlights into the windows of the house—most of whom were not even members. This practice left me quite unsettled.

My extroverted friends would say, "Oh, Brian, that's a wonderful ministry opportunity!" Maybe so. But extroverts do not understand the need for us introverts to have personal time to ourselves. When introverts are constantly bombarded by noise and people, introverts begin to feel as if they are jabbed with hot pokers. Anxiety sets in. Anger, agitation, or emotional outbursts may follow. Understand that it is not that introverts do not want to minister and help people. Rather, introverts require time to recoup from social events.[1]

Nonetheless, the feeling of homesickness did not leave. It worsened and intensified beyond the feelings experienced while living in Yadkinville. Since that time, we built a house that feels more like home. Even though this house feels more like home than any other house in which we have lived, there is still a sense of ongoing homesickness when considering the family and friends who passed, and the ongoing sense of disassociation I find with modern society. The older I get, the more I feel like a stranger. Or maybe it is just that I am becoming stranger with age. I will let you be the judge.

While contemplating these issues, it seems that we all may suffer from a sense of homesickness. Our ultimate homesickness stems from the understanding that this world is not our home. Something beyond our current state of existence must be better. Surely there must be a place where no suffering is found—a place of peace and contentment. This homesickness is rooted in our desire and longing for heaven.

Solomon[2] acknowledged our desire and longing for heaven as he writes, "[God] has also put eternity in their hearts, but no one can discover the work God has done from beginning to end" (Ecc. 3:11).[3] Solomon understood that human beings are temporal and finite. Yet, within them is found a spiritual longing for the eternal. Humans have an innate hole in their being that can only be filled with the awesome presence of God. In like manner, humans have a homesickness for a land of peace and tranquility that only can be satisfied by a heavenly home.

Heaven is home for both God and his people. Heaven is the home that we desire. It is the place of belonging that we so cherish. Combining

---

1. While Jesus was most likely an ambivert (both introverted and extroverted), he required time to himself to recuperate from the times that he was inundated with crowds of people. See Mark 1:35–38. Interestingly, some have claimed that Jesus could have been introverted for this very reason.

2. As a traditionalist concerning the writers of Scripture, I hold that Solomon wrote the majority, if not all, of the book of Ecclesiastes. Good evidence suggests that Ecclesiastes originated during the time of Solomon. Considering that the book identifies the teacher of the book, or Qoheleth, as the "son of David, king in Jerusalem" (Ecc. 1:1), it is not a far stretch to claim that Solomon authored the book.

3. Unless otherwise noted, all quoted Scripture comes from the Christian Standard Bible (Nashville: Holman, 2020).

truths from Isaiah 52:15[4] and Isaiah 64:4,[5] Paul contends that "What no eye has seen, no ear has heard, and no human heart has conceived—God has prepared these things for those who love him" (1 Cor. 2:9). Later, the apostle writes that "For our momentary light affliction is producing for us an absolutely incomparable eternal weight of glory. So we do not focus on what is seen, but on what is unseen. For what is seen is temporary, but what is unseen is eternal" (2 Cor. 4:17–18). Despite our problems and afflictions, they will pale in comparison to the eternal glory that will be experienced in our heavenly home.

## Questions about Heaven

While serving as pastor of Huntsville Baptist Church in Yadkinville, North Carolina, I was met by a woman in her seventies who wanted to speak with me about the messages I had been preaching on heaven. Her name was Sandy Riddle. Sandy was a wonderful, hard-working woman who loved her family and friends. However, she had been met with many struggles in life, leading her to sometimes become a bit standoffish to those she did not know well.

Sandy wondered whether she would truly have a place in heaven. She knew that she was saved. But having been hurt by legalistic Christians in the past, she wondered whether she would enjoy heaven. She feared that she might be disappointed with heaven, and that God would kick her out due to her displeasure. She had been led to believe that heaven was one big church service with constant singing and preaching. She sincerely said, "Brian, I think that would get boring after a while." I responded, "You know, I think it would, too." I then responded that heaven would be far more active and superior to the prognostications that have been made by individuals behind their pulpits on Sunday mornings. We will dive into the depths of these conversations throughout the book.

During our conversations, Sandy posed a question that haunts me to this day. She earnestly asked me, "Brian, do you think there will be a place in heaven for someone like me?" Even now while writing her question, my

4. "So [God] will sprinkle many nations. Kings will shut their mouths because of him, for they will see what had not been told them, and they will understand, what they had not heard" (Isa. 52:15).

5. "From ancient times no one has heard, no one has listened to, no eye has seen any God except you who acts on behalf of the one who waits for him" (Isa. 64:4).

throat begins to tighten, and I find myself fighting back tears. I replied, "If you have trusted Jesus with your salvation, you most certainly will have a place in heaven. Jesus did not come to grant heaven to those who think they are super-spiritual and overly religious. Jesus often combatted those who thought they were holier than everyone else. He came to provide us with a way to come home. That home is heaven."

Sandy seemed to be much more optimistic about heaven after our conversations. Ironically, Sandy's questions correlated greatly with a series of messages I delivered at Huntsville Baptist Church. This book consists of both the conversations that I had with Sandy and the material that was included in the sermon series that I taught at the time. To date, I have only delivered those messages once. Now, you have access to the series in this book.

In full disclosure, it should be disclosed that a great deal of additional research has gone into the writing of this book. While the messages in historic Huntsville, North Carolina, and my conversations with Sandy are the basis of this book, some areas have been greatly expanded due to the accessibility of additional resources unavailable at the time. My exposure to the works of Thomas Aquinas, Anselm of Canterbury, and the early church fathers has expanded and intensified my view of heaven. Moreover, I like to think that I obtained greater research skills after acquiring a Ph.D. since the time that this research was first compiled. About 5 years have elapsed from the time that these conversations first occurred to the final publication of this book. Nonetheless, I digress.

While I did not realize it at the time, a common thread was found in my conversations with Sandy and the sermon series delivered that fateful summer of 2018. That thread was that heaven is a place far greater than anything we could ever imagine. Sandy had a preconceived notion that heaven would be something less than the ultimate good. This brings us to the central message of this book. The purpose of this book is based on a related concept devised by Anselm of Canterbury (1033–1109). Anselm argues in his book *Proslogium* that God is "a being than which nothing greater can be conceived."[6] Anselm's argumentation is known in the apologetics world as the ontological argument. While the ontological argument has been dismissed by some modern apologists, the argument has grown in its scope and power in my mind. Even if the argument does not move

---

6. Anselm, *Proslogium* 2, 7.

the unbeliever to belief, Anselm's argument speaks to the nature of God existing as the greatest possible Being.[7] Anselm writes,

> And so, Lord, do thou, who dost give understanding to faith, give me, so far as thou knowest it to be profitable, to understand that thou art as we believe; and that thou art that which we believe. And, indeed, we believe that thou art a being than which nothing greater can be conceived. Or is there no such nature, since the fool hath said in his heart, there is no God? (Psalms 14:1). But, at any rate, this very fool, when he hears of this being of which I speak—a being than which nothing greater can be conceived—understands what he hears, and what he understands is in his understanding; although he does not understand it to exist.
>
> For, it is one thing for an object to be in the understanding, and another to understand that the object exists. When a painter first conceives of what he will afterwards perform, he has it in his understanding, but he does not yet understand it to be, because he has not yet performed it. But after he has made the painting, he both has it in his understanding, and he understands that it exists, because he has made it.
>
> Hence, even the fool is convinced that something exists in the understanding, at least, than which nothing greater can be conceived. For, when he hears of this, he understands it. And whatever is understood, exists in the understanding. And assuredly that, than which nothing greater can be conceived, cannot exist in the understanding alone. For, suppose it exists in the understanding alone: then it can be conceived to exist in reality; which is greater.
>
> Therefore, if that, than which nothing greater can be conceived, exists in the understanding alone, the very being, than which nothing greater can be conceived, is one, than which a greater can be conceived. But obviously this is impossible. Hence, there is no doubt that there exists a being, than which nothing greater can be conceived, and it exists both in the understanding and in reality.[8]

The maximally great God who is perfect in every way is often identified as the Anselmian God by many modern philosophers.[9] The crux of Christian theism is built around the concept of the Anselmian God—God existing as the God of the Omni's (omnipotent, omniscient, omnipresent, and omnibenevolent). Now, this leads us to the core thesis of the book. If

---

7. Otherwise known as a Maximally Great Being.

8. Anselm, *Proslogium* 2, 7–8.

9. Baggett and Walls, *Good God*, 51–52.

God is known as a maximally great Being, as understood by the concept of the Anselmian God, then it stands to reason that the heaven that this maximally great God prepares for his children will be a maximally great place.

Therefore, if God is a being than which nothing greater could be conceived and heaven is the greatest gift that God gives his people, then it stands to reason that heaven is that place than which nowhere greater could be conceived. Worded another way, heaven, therefore, is a place than which nothing greater could be conceived, since it is the greatest place granted by a God than which nothing greater could be conceived. Thus, the goal of this book is to show that heaven is going to be an exciting, wonderful, fun-filled place where everyone will be loved, appreciated, valued, and, thereby, people will discover their ultimate home.

Heaven is not going to be one long church service. Rather, heaven will be a place bustling with activity while also allowing its citizens to enjoy the serenity, peace, and joy that they could never hope to experience in this life. In addition, it is my hope that anyone reading this material would no longer fear death and dismiss any idea that heaven would be a place where they would feel excluded. Heaven is the home we all long to have.

Heaven is going to be far greater than your greatest thoughts about heaven. Think of the greatest home you have ever had. Heaven will be far greater and grander than the home you identified. As previously noted, the concept of the Anselmian God is that God is "that than which nothing greater can be thought."[10] If God is greater than anything that we can perceive about him, then heaven will be greater than anything you can consider about the heavenly home we have awaiting us. However, because of the problems of life, our conceptions of heaven are often diminished. It could be objected that even the thoughts presented in this book about heaven are inadequate. In this case, the objector would be correct. Nonetheless, if the reader's concepts about heaven are expanded by this work, then it will have been successful.

Three final points need to be made before getting into the material. Before I preached the sermon series on heaven, I asked the people of Huntsville Baptist Church—the church I served while preaching this series—to provide me with a list of questions they had about heaven. I also asked people online to post their questions about heaven, too. After taking the poll, I compiled a list of the most frequently asked questions about heaven to consider when constructing the sermon series. While the focus

10. Anselm, *Proslogion* V, 104.

of the book is on my conversation with Sandy Riddle, much of the material that was discussed with Sandy was the result of my research for the sermon series. The questions found in the book are not listed in a top ten order according to the poll—that is, the tenth chapter does not necessarily indicate the most asked question. In case you are wondering, the most asked question about heaven concerned the inclusion of pets and animals in heaven. While this question does not get an individual chapter devoted to it, this issue is covered in great detail in Chapter 5.

The questions are also not listed according to Sandy's level of frequency, these questions were among the most asked questions by people in general. Ironically, Sandy's questions were found to match the questions that had been included in the polls, indicating that these are the kinds of questions about heaven that capture the imagination of the general populace.

Finally, I have been told over the years that we should not predict what heaven will be like. I find this attitude quite unfortunate. Scripture offers clues that help us peer into deeper theological and ontological realities. By using the practice of abductive reasoning—the practice of observing materials and then finding the simplest and most likely conclusion from the observations—a person can logically adduce (or abduce) certain conclusions from the biblical material given. For instance, the word *trinity* is not found in the biblical text. However, from the baptism of Jesus, the expositor notes that the Father speaks from heaven (Matt. 3:17), the Spirit descends like a dove (Matt. 3:16), all while Jesus the Son is baptized (Matt. 3:16–17). Given the references identifying the divine nature of the three,[11] one can adduce that the Trinity exists. Abductive reasoning draws varying probabilities but may not always offer certainties. The evidence for the Trinity is far greater than some of the conclusions drawn in this text. Nonetheless, I believe that the answers given in this book find good Scriptural backing. One thing is for sure, heaven will be far greater than any of us could ever imagine! Heaven will be a place than which nothing greater can be conceived.

---

11. The Father is confirmed as God throughout the OT and NT (Gen. 1; Exod. 3:14). The Son is identified as God in the flesh (John 1:1–3; Heb. 1:3). The Spirit is also identified as God (Acts 5:3–4; 1 Cor. 2:10–12).

## Chapter One

# WHERE IS HEAVEN LOCATED? (PART ONE)

## *2 Corinthians 5:1–10*

1. *Presently Located in a Divine State (2 Cor. 5:1, 8).*

2. *Presently Located in a Spiritual State (2 Cor. 5:2–5; 2 Cor. 12:2–4).*

3. *Presently Located in a Living State (2 Cor. 5:6–10).*

FRANCES LEGG IS A woman that every pastor desires to have as a congregant—although Rev. Dennis Shaw may disagree. Dennis preceded me as the pastor of Huntsville Baptist Church. Dennis and I are good friends to this day. Dennis and Frances were natured very similarly. Where I am a bit more reserved in disposition, Frances and Dennis were quite the opposite. They proved to be the life of the party. Each of them alone could light up a room. However, when Dennis and Frances got together, sparks would fly. Bystanders were assured to be given the show of a lifetime as Dennis and Frances have a longstanding partnership in giving each other a hard time. It is enjoyable to sit back and see how one will try to get a leg up (no pun intended) on the other. If these encounters occurred during a church meal, one would be treated to a dinner and a show. If a person left with a soured disposition after being around these two, then it would only prove that the person's funny bone was broken.

Though Frances was normally gregarious, on this fateful day, Frances approached me with an unusual sigh on her face. Frances said to me, "Brian, I need to talk to you for a minute." Usually, conversations that begin in that manner take much longer than one minute. She continued, "Sandy is not doing the best physically. She seems to be afraid of dying. Sandy has many questions she has been asking me about your messages. I keep asking her, 'Why don't you just talk to the preacher?' She always tells me, 'He wouldn't want to hear what I have to say,' but I always tell her, 'Well, you won't know unless you ask him.'"

I replied, "I'd be happy to speak with her." Frances smiled and said, "Would you? I would greatly appreciate it. I'll be sure to let Sandy know." I added, "Does Sandy have a day that she would like for me to visit?" Frances added, "Well, Sandy may prefer a phone call to a personal visit." I concluded, "Let her know that I will be available whenever she would like to talk."

The sanctuary of Huntsville Baptist Church normally sparkles with an assortment of colors as the rays of the sun dance through the shimmering stained-glass windows of the old country church. The white walls of the church and the green carpet added extra flavor to the rainbow-saturated light display. However, on this overcast day, the sun was unable to put on the spectacle that normally accompanied daylight. It was on this dreary day that Sandy called me. I had headed back toward the office after delivering the paperwork for the Wednesday night Bible study which normally occurred in the fellowship building. The educational wing comprised both the office and Sunday school classes and was found on one side of the church, whereas the fellowship building was found on the other wing. The sanctuary separated the educational wing from the fellowship building. To get from one to the other, a person needed to either walk through the sanctuary or travel behind the sanctuary where the baptismal was found. If a person were to observe the church from the front, the fellowship building would be found on the left, the sanctuary in the middle, and the educational wing on the right. Wednesday night studies were a treat at Huntsville as we enjoyed an informal setting for our studies replete with discussions, coffee, and an occasional box of Krispy Kreme doughnuts. On this day, I had left the fellowship building and entered the sanctuary when Sandy called.

My phone rang, and I answered. Sandy said with a tinge of nervousness in her voice, "Pastor, do you have a few minutes to talk to me about heaven?"

"Sure, Sandy! I would love to speak with you anytime."

She continued with a bit of reserve. "Preacher, I don't want you to think badly of me. Because some of my questions may sound a bit strange. You might think that I am a heathen for asking some of these things."

I said, "Sandy, your questions are always welcome." I then told her about how I had become an agnostic at one point. I assured her that as God had brought me back into the Christian faith and the apologetic ministry, if I didn't have the answers, then I would search until I found them. Sandy said with a bit of reassurance, "Thank you so much for your understanding."

Sandy's first question was to the point. She was not one to beat around the bush. She asked, "Brian, some people say that when we die, we are dead. We don't go to heaven or hell. We are just dead. Why can't death be like that? Why do we have to go anywhere? Can we be sure that we will live on in heaven after we die? Where is heaven anyway?" Admittedly, I was a bit shocked to a degree. Most people I have encountered are more fearful of death being an ultimate finality rather than considering that life continues. However, the more I have thought about Sandy's opening question, the more I can understand her perspective. When a person has been hurt, sleep is a respite. The person is not bothered by anyone or anything. For the residents of the Nazi concentration camps, sleep was the only occasion when one could escape the daily horrors. However, if one considers that heaven is the best possible place that can be conceived, then its existence is of the utmost hope and consolation. I then related her question to 2 Corinthians 5 and Revelation 21 which we will cover in this chapter.

Sandy's questions were deep and profound. This was no surprise because Sandy was a deep-thinking woman. Does a person continue to live after one has taken their final breath? Can we know where heaven is located? When polling individuals concerning their questions about heaven, I was surprised to find that many people wanted to know where heaven was located. God has often been called "The Man Upstairs." People want to know whether God was a man looking over people like the gray-haired, gray-bearded man portrayed in the Sistine Chapel. Can heaven be reached by taking a rocket to some spatial corner of the cosmos?

This chapter will show that the answer is a bit more complicated than one might think. Presently, heaven is in the spiritual realm where God resides. When a person dies, they will enter into this spiritual realm. However, the future heaven state of heaven will be a bit different. The new heaven and the new earth are going to be a new creation that will merge the spiritual and physical realms into one. The believer's existence will only get better and better with God. Only God could take heaven and make it better. But that is what we see that the Bible suggests.

I read the humorous, fictional story of three men who approached the gates of heaven. They were immediately greeted by Saint Peter. "Hello. My name is Peter. Welcome to the Kingdom of God! In heaven we have but one rule: DO NOT step on a duck." One of the three men replied, "I'm sorry. Can you repeat that?" Peter said, "Over the years, many misconceptions of heaven have arisen. Yes, it's a pretty nice place. But there's one problem— the ducks. If you step on a duck, it will begin to quack. Then, all the other ducks will begin to quack, and it's simply a nuisance for us all. So, if you step on a duck, you must suffer the consequences." The three men looked at each other, laughed it off, and continued into heaven.

As far as the eye could see, ducks were seen everywhere. Almost immediately, one of the men accidentally stepped on a duck. Just as Peter had said, the duck began to quack, and then a tidal wave of ducks arose. Soon after the quacks had subsided, Saint Peter approached the men in hand with a very unpleasant woman. Without a word, he shackled the woman to the man that stepped on the duck and left.

The other two men were careful not to step on a duck. Although they tried their best, one of them eventually stepped on a duck. The same phenomenon occurred, and Saint Peter arrived again with a huge Amazonian woman who was rippling with muscles. He shackled the woman to the second man and left.

The final man trod with care and spent many days and nights successfully stepping around the ducks. After a while, Saint Peter approached the man with the most beautiful woman he had ever seen. He shackled the woman to the man and left without a word. The man was so delighted that he audibly said to himself, "Wow, what did I do to deserve this?" The woman replied, "I don't know what you did, but I stepped on a duck." Thankfully, the real heaven will not have ducks to worry with.

Is heaven a real place? Do we have to fear the onslaught of ducks and being bound to an attractive or unattractive person? While the latter is not a serious question one should consider, the reality of the soul's existence past death is no laughing matter. Differing theological opinions provide very different views about what happens to a person after death.

The time between a person's death and the final resurrection is called the *intermediate state* by theologians. It is called "intermediate" because it is the period that is transitionary between one's existence in the afterlife before the resurrection as opposed to one's existence after the resurrection. The key question surrounds whether the soul can exist independently from the body in a disembodied state. As Millard Erickson notes, "Every view of the intermediate state is, of course, closely related to a specific anthropology or understanding of human nature."[1]

Theologians are divided into numerous camps when considering the disembodied existence of a human being. First, some hold to *soul cessationism* or *soul mortality*. Individuals in this camp hold to a form of neo-orthodoxy which holds that the whole perception of the immortal soul is a Greek concept rather than a Jewish one. The body is held to be a monistic unity, thereby eliminating any dualistic notion of an immortal soul. Thus, there is no separation of the soul from the body. Therefore, no part of a person survives death.[2] Some movements teach that a person's soul ceases to exist at death.[3] But how does one reconcile the concept of soul mortality with the Scriptural indicators that the soul survives death? Quite honestly, as I will show, you cannot.

Second, individuals within Seventh-day Adventism and the Jehovah's Witness movement hold to the concept of *soul sleep*.[4] In this view, the soul does not cease to exist, per se, but it does not live in a conscious state either. Rather, the soul sleeps until the time of the resurrection. According to Seventh-day Adventists, "the condition of man in death is one of unconsciousness [and that] all men, good and evil alike, remain in the grave from death to the resurrection."[5] Adherents to soul sleep take passages that mention the rest of the spirit literally (1 Cor. 15:6, 18, 20, 51; 1 Thess. 4:13–15). Problematic for the soul sleep position is that Scripture indicates the active presence of the soul after death as we shall see in the forthcoming passage of Scripture.

Third, some hold to the idea of *purgatory*. Primarily, the view of purgatory is held in Roman Catholic circles. Within Roman Catholicism, it is believed that the soul of a person is judged at death. The person is either granted immediate access to heaven, condemned to hell, or given time to

---

1. Erickson, *Christian Theology,* 1079.

2. Brunner, *Christian Doctrine,* 383–85, 408–14.

3. I have been amazed to find that some theologians even teach this concept which is bizarre considering the wealth of biblical information that suggests that the soul survives death.

4. Some early Anabaptists and Socinians also held this view.

5. *Seventh-Day Adventists Answer Questions,* 13.

purge away accumulated sins before being allowed to access heaven. Joseph Pohle writes that the soul is "moved of its own accord to hasten either to Heaven, or Hell, or Purgatory, according to its desserts."[6] The problem with this view is that there are no biblical passages related to the concept of purgatory.[7] The only possibility is the Judgment Seat of Christ (1 Cor. 3:15).[8] Although even here, it is apparent that a person's works are tried and not the person's soul.

Fourth, a creative view that the soul instantly travels to the time of the resurrection is called *instantaneous resurrection.*[9] W. D. Davies advocated this view in his book *Paul and Rabbinic Judaism.*[10] The idea behind this view is that the soul automatically transcends time at death to enter the resurrected age. Thus, what seems to have been a moment to the person who died may have in reality spanned several hundred if not thousands of years. I like to think of this as the anesthesia view. Anyone who has been put to sleep knows that when one reawakens it seems like only a few moments have passed when a good deal of time has passed in reality. The problem with this view is that it is a creative spin on the soul sleep position. Thus, the same problems that apply to the soul sleep position are found with the instantaneous resurrection stance.

In contrast to the previous four views, the fifth view is called *soul survival.* It is the position that the soul survives death in a conscious, living state. When taken at face value, Paul argues that the believer does not cease to exist at death, but rather enters a new spiritual state in the presence of God. This is the view that I hold and will defend. Why? Paul and other biblical writers hold to the soul survival position. While the Bible does not explicitly describe the spiritual state of human existence with as vivid descriptions that may be preferred, the ongoing theme throughout the entirety of Scripture indicates that human beings are made with a divine image that survives the finite mode of existence of our fleshly bodies. This is not only a Grecian position, but a thoroughly Hebraic position as well. As

---

6. Pohle, *Catholic Doctrine of the Last Things*, 18.

7. See Gentry, *Absent from the Body,* for a fantastic rebuttal against the purgatory viewpoint.

8. The only other possible exception is found in the apocryphal book 2 Macc 12:43–45.

9. Erickson, *Christian Theology,* 1083.

10. Davies, *Paul and Rabbinic Judaism,* 317–18.

we will note, Genesis and even the pessimistic book of Ecclesiastes denote the spiritual state of existence that survives death.

While the Bible presents a form of a dualism of body and soul, biblical writers do not dismiss the physical world as the ancient Gnostics did. God has plans to recreate the entire cosmos. John, in the book of Revelation, reveals that the spiritual state is not the end of the story for creation either. For there will be a new heaven and a new earth that will be created after Christ's millennial reign. God is in a state of resurrecting all of creation to a perfect state of balance and unity. Spiritual and physical entities will unite in a fashion that has only been experienced by the resurrected Jesus. Being the firstfruits of our resurrection, as Jesus was raised, so we will, and so will creation.

Thus, to answer the question of where heaven is located, we must first look to 2 Corinthians 5:1–10 to identify the present location of heaven as we defend the soul survival position. Afterward, we will examine the location of heaven as it occurs in the final state of a new heaven and a new earth for all eternity. The first five verses of Revelation 21 will be our focal point at that time.

Where does a believing person go when they die? This was a question with which my wife and I met firsthand. My grandfather, Rev. Odell Sisk, died in 2016. Grandpa had been a pastor for most of his life and all of mine. After Grandpa passed, my son asked me and my wife, "Where is great-grandpa now?" We told him, "He is in heaven, honey." This led to an interesting conversation about life, death, and the afterlife.

Many people ask the same question that my son Grayson posed. Where does a person go when they die? That is, are individuals conscious and aware of their disembodied state? In Paul's second letter to the Corinthian church, the apostle provides three descriptions of the location of heaven before the resurrection. Paul argues that heaven is a divine, spiritual, and living place.

## Presently Located in a Divine State (2 Cor. 5:1, 8)

Directing his attention to the believer, Paul teaches that if a person's "earthly tent is destroyed" (5:1) which describes a person's body, then the deceased person still has a "building from God" (5:1). Paul had in mind the sojourning tent life where one moved their tents from one location to another.[11] Thus, Paul holds that the earthly tent is an individual's body. The building from God likely refers to the person's future resurrected body, but it could also denote a person's heavenly state. However, this is a topic of great debate among commentators, as there are at least seven interpretations of this passage.[12]

Regardless of how one interprets 2 Corinthians 5:1, Paul leaves no room for doubt concerning the divine spiritual state in verse 8 where he contends that when a believer is absent from the body—that is, when they have died—the believer is then "at home with the Lord" (5:8). Perhaps, Paul had in mind Solomon's teachings in Ecclesiastes about a person's soul returning to God. It is also possible he had in mind his own near-death experience which will be discussed in a later chapter. Nonetheless, Paul most certainly held that a person who died would not cease to exist, but he or she would be escorted into the divine presence of God.

Paul is not the only biblical writer that held that the soul consciously survived death and was escorted to the presence of God. While many passages could be offered, three texts are especially noteworthy. First, Solomon confirms the intermediate state. Surprisingly for some, the Old Testament, which does not mention the afterlife in as great detail as the New Testament does, indicates that a person enters into the presence of God upon one's departure from this earth. As mentioned earlier, the Teacher of Ecclesiastes (i.e., Solomon) notes,

> Also, they are afraid of heights and dangers on the road; the almond tree blossoms, the grasshopper loses its spring, and the caper berry has no effect; for the mere mortal is headed to his eternal home, and mourners will walk around in the street; before the silver cord is snapped, and the gold bowl is broken, and the jar is shattered at the spring, and the wheel is broken into the well, and the dust returns to the earth as it once was, and the spirit returns to God who gave it (Ecc. 12:5–7).

11. "Tent life is a ready metaphor for humankind's brief sojourn in the world, and it depicts 'the instability, and thus the vulnerability, of one's moral existence." Garland, 2 *Corinthians*, 249.

12. The seven interpretations include: 1. The building of John 14:2 which includes many rooms. Hodge, *Exposition of the Second Epistle*, 485–88. 2. A reference to the body of Christ. Robinson, *Body*, 76; Ellis, "II Corinthians v.1–10 in Pauline Eschatology," 217–18. 3. Another view interprets the building to be the heavenly temple. Hanhart, *Intermediate State*, 160–61. 4. The building is an intermediate heavenly body. 5. The inner, or spiritual man. 6. The resurrected body of Jesus. 7. Metaphorically referencing the glory of the millennial age. Furnish, *II Corinthians*, 294–95.

Notice the language of the Teacher. The body returns to dust, whereas the spirit returns to God. In my estimation, this addresses the intermediate state—a state where the soul is enjoined with God. This leads us to ask, what state of being is this intermediate state? The Teacher, most likely Solomon himself, has in mind an even earlier biblical text.[13] In Genesis 2:7, God "formed the man out of the dust from the ground and breathed the breath of life into his nostrils, and the man became a living being." God is the source of all life. But by making humanity in his image, he gifted humanity with a living soul.

Second, Jesus's parable of the rich man and Lazarus also teaches that the righteous go before the presence of God upon death (Luke 16:19–31). While a full exposition of the passage is not possible at this juncture, it is important to note that Jesus fully accepts that righteous individuals enter paradise, deemed "Abraham's side" (16:22).[14] Abraham's side was a place that Jesus identified as a spiritual state of existence.[15] Lazarus was alive and was present beside Abraham. One would hold that he was also in the presence of God. It may be contended that the righteous did not have full access to God in this spiritual state of heaven until Jesus's work was accomplished on the cross. However, I do not know that we have adequate information on either side to make such a conclusive statement. When considering Solomon's lesson in Ecclesiastes, it would seem like the righteous went in the presence of God to at least some degree at this time.

Third, Jesus's teaching in John 11:25 strongly alludes to a person's existence after death. Jesus spoke with Mary and Martha, the sisters of Lazarus who had died. Martha inquired of Jesus why he did not arrive earlier. If he had arrived sooner, their brother would not have died because Jesus could have healed him. Jesus looked at Martha and told her that Lazarus would rise again (11:23). Thinking he was speaking of the final resurrection, Martha assured Jesus that she knew that Lazarus would rise again on the last day. Jesus then corrected Martha's theology by saying, "I am the resurrection and the life. The one who believes in me, even if he dies, will live. Everyone who lives and believes in me will never die. Do you believe

---

13. I hold to the traditional understanding of biblical authorship. That is, I assume that Solomon wrote the books ascribed to him and that Moses wrote the vast majority of the Torah.

14. Also translated as "Abraham's bosom."

15. "Abraham's side" apparently refers to a place of paradise for Old Testament believers at the time of death (cf. Luke 23:43; 2 Cor. 12:3." Walvoord and Zuck, *Bible Knowledge Commentary*, 247.

this?" (11:25–26). For Jesus's teaching to be accurate, soul survival must be true. Jesus did not indicate that the child of God would live, die, and then live again. Rather, he said that the believer would never truly die but continuously live.

The Scripture indicates that a person does not cease to exist at death but continues to live on in the afterlife. I once spoke with a woman whom we will call Marci. Marci was distraught because her husband had died. Marci told me that her husband had accepted Christ and had lived faithfully as a believer for many years. However, some individuals in her family had told her that she must not think that her husband was still alive. They contended that the Bible did not teach that a person's soul lived past death. The family member held that such a view stemmed from pagan Greek philosophy rather than biblical theology.

Marci asked me with a tear in her eye, "Pastor, is my husband still living?" I assured her by the authority of God's Word that if her husband had accepted Christ, then he was very much alive. I shared with her the passages of Scripture that I shared with you just now. Marci hugged me and thanked me for sharing these Scriptures with her. She said, "You know, I always thought that my husband was still alive in heaven. However, not knowing the Scripture that well, I did not know if my family member was correct. I thought I may have been wishing for something that was not true." We can take great comfort in knowing that our loved ones are with God. Furthermore, soul survival alleviates the fears one may hold with their own mortality.

## Presently Located in a Spiritual State
### (2 Cor. 5:2–5; 2 Cor. 12:2–4)

In verses 2–5, Paul describes how individuals desire to be clothed (being with a body) but are found naked (without a body) at death. In verse 4, Paul denotes his preference for the final resurrected state.[16] This tells us that while the spiritual state is wondrous and exciting, it does not represent the final state. The resurrected body is the end goal as it will combine

---

16. Surprisingly, some commentators believe that Paul describes the believer receiving a resurrected body at death. However, how is it that the resurrection is described at Christ's return in 1 Thessalonians? It makes no sense. I am surprised at the rejection of an intermediate state. Not only is the intermediate state implied, but it is also pretty clear in the text.

the benefits of both the spiritual and earthly dimensions into a new form. Where is this spiritual state found?

In 2 Corinthians 12:2–4, Paul discusses what many believe to have been his near-death experience where he was taken to the "third heaven" (12:2, 4). James Davis notes, "Paul relates an experience which happened to him some fourteen years earlier (placing it in the period between his first visit to Jerusalem following his conversion and his arrival in Antioch [Acts 9:23–30; 11:19–26])."[17] David K. Lowery of the *Bible Knowledge Commentary* notes, "Paul's indirect reference to himself as a man in Christ showed that he regarded this great experience not as a consequence of inherent worthiness or spiritual excellence but because he was 'in Christ.' As such it anticipated what everyone in Christ will one day experience, the presence of Christ in heaven."[18] Thus, while Paul is speaking of himself in the third person, he is undoubtedly speaking of himself. Most likely, this experience occurred around AD 37 to 39 during his escape from Damascus.[19]

Paul delivers firsthand information concerning the third heaven, noting that the third heaven is something of a spiritual dimension. The first heaven is the earth's atmosphere; the second heaven is the universe; and the third heaven is the spiritual dimension that serves as the residence of God, angelic beings, and saints who have passed beforehand.

For some, spiritual beings seem like some esoteric notion of thoughts, ideas, and concepts, but nothing that exists in reality. However, a person should remember that the Bible teaches about the existence of the Holy Spirit—the third Person of the Triune Godhead. Furthermore, Jesus indicates that God is spirit (John 4:24). Angelic beings are shown throughout Scripture to be spiritual beings, including the fallen demonic beings (Eph. 6:12).[20] Thus, if one is to suggest that the idea of spiritual beings living outside of a physical body is a Grecian philosophical concept, then the interpreter must explain how spiritual entities—including God himself—exist outside of a physical form. Soul mortality simply does not work.

17. Elwell, *Evangelical Commentary on the Bible*, 995.

18. Walvoord and Zuck, *Bible Knowledge Commentary*, 582.

19. "This places it relatively close to the escape from Damascus, which must have occurred between 37 and 39. In both cases, Paul reports events from the early, relatively unknown years of his apostolic mission, while he was in Tarsus. The revelation was given to him when he was a nobody." Seifrid, *Second Letter to the Corinthians*, 438.

20. Demons are fallen angels. Their difference with angels of heaven is in service and not their identity. That is, angels serve God, whereas demons serve Satan. Both angels and demons are spiritual beings.

Currently, heaven consists of a spiritual state. Jesus is the only one who has a resurrected body right now. However, later, when Christ returns, everyone's spirit will be reunited with their bodies. Paul states,

> For if we believe that Jesus died and rose again, in the same way, through Jesus, God will bring with him those who have fallen asleep (metaphorically referencing those who are in the presence of God). For we say to you by a word from the Lord: We who are still alive at the Lord's coming will certainly not precede those who have fallen asleep. For the Lord himself will descend from heaven with a shout, with the archangel's voice, and with the trumpet of God, and the dead in Christ will rise first. Then we who are alive, who are left, will be caught up together with them in the clouds to meet the Lord in the air, and so we will always be with the Lord. Therefore encourage one another with these words (1 Thess. 4:14–18).

When we bury our loved ones, do not think that their body is gone forever. When Christ returns, their bodies will rise just as Jesus's body did. Everyone in Christ will experience their own Easter moment.

## Presently Located in a Living State (2 Cor. 5:6–10)

This spiritual state is not a deadened state but a living one. As we have already mentioned, paradise, or the spiritual heaven, is a divine spiritual location for those who have received Christ. Paul discussed his near-death experience (NDE) when he was taken to the third heaven. Paul then contrasts the physical and spiritual states in three different ways.

First, while a person is in the body, they are away from the presence of the Lord (2 Cor. 5:6). Theologically, we know that God is always with us. There is never a place where God is not. However, Paul contends that one cannot fully experience God while in the physical body. This is something that Paul must have learned during his experience outside the body.

Second, Paul notes that believers cannot currently see God due to the restraints of the physical dimension. This should not be surprising for two reasons. First, scientifically, it is said that human beings cannot see but a portion of wavelengths that exist. The human eye cannot detect radio frequencies or infrared wavelengths. On the other side of the spectrum, the human eye cannot see x-rays or gamma rays. Give my apologies to Bruce Banner. Rather, human beings can only detect a small fragment of wavelengths that represent our color spectrum. Because of this, I think it is highly likely that heaven will contain colors that we cannot now see. Second, theologically, God has hidden himself for numerous reasons. Perhaps the greatest reason is for our protection. Peter explains that when God steps into space-time with full force, the elements of creation will pass away (2 Pet. 3:9). While the Christian now lives by faith in God's ultimate reality, faith will give way to sight when a person enters the spiritual abode of God's powerful, majestic presence.

Finally, Paul flips the argument made in the first point to say that being absent from this body is to enter the presence of God. (2 Cor. 5:8). For to be absent from this body is to be present with God. Thus, a person does not cease to exist at death. Rather, a person is more alive than ever before.

Consider what Paul stated a chapter earlier. He said, "Therefore, we do not give up. Even though our outer person is being destroyed, our inner person is being renewed day by day. For our momentary light affliction is producing for us an absolutely incomparable eternal weight of glory" (2 Cor. 4:16–18). Just what kind of hardships had they endured? In Paul's own words, "Five times I received the forty lashes minus one from the Jews. Three times I was beaten with rods. Once I received a stoning. Three times I was shipwrecked. I have spent a night and a day in the open sea" (2 Cor. 11:24–25). Despite all these problems, Paul believed that they were building an "incomparable eternal weight of glory" (2 Cor. 4:18). Knowing that there is a living state beyond this mortal realm gave Paul hope. It should do the same for us, too.

Concerning the living state of spiritual existence, Jesus also shows the living state of life after death by telling the man on the cross, "Truly I tell you, today you will be with me in paradise" (Lk. 23:43). The following may sound a bit stern, but I think it is true. Advocates of soul cessationism, soul sleep, and instantaneous resurrection make Jesus out to be a liar.[21] Only the soul survival construct can account for Jesus's promise that the thief on the cross would be with Jesus in paradise on the day of both men's death. In contrast to soul cessationism, Jesus did not say, "Truly I tell you, one day you will be with me in the new creation." In contrast to soul sleep, Jesus did not say, "Truly I tell you, after you rest for an indeterminate period, you

---

21. I do not include the purgatory view because it is possible that one could claim that the thief on the cross was granted instant access to heaven, whereas others may be forced to spend time in purgatory. But one could also argue that the thief had a lot of sins to have atoned which would make his time in purgatory feasible. Nevertheless, such an argument is beyond the scope of this work.

will be resurrected." Neither did Jesus say, "Truly I tell you, today your soul will be automatically transported to the future final resurrection where you will be with me in the new creation." Rather, Jesus promised that the thief would consciously and spiritually see him in the spiritual state of paradise that very day—the day of his death.

Near-death experiences (NDEs) provide extra-biblical evidence that the soul survives death.[22] One telling example is an instance recorded by Gary Habermas and J. P. Moreland in their book *Beyond Death*. According to Habermas and Moreland, a 1982 Gallup poll revealed that 15 percent of respondents admitted having experienced an NDE—which translates to around twenty-three million Americans![23] We are not talking about a few people having these types of experiences. Twenty-three million Americans have described conscious experiences with God and others after having died. Granted, some stories may be difficult to swallow. Disembodied experiences that occur on the other side of eternity cannot be verified scientifically. Yet, that does not mean that they are not true. Similar stories from different people across the world may weigh in favor of such experiences. However, for our purposes, disembodied experiences that can be proven in our space and time can implicate that the soul survives death. One may assume that such cases are rare. But with an estimated twenty-three million Americans as noted by Habermas and Moreland, not even considering global occurrences (which would increase the number of NDEs exponentially), such occurrences are surprisingly commonplace.[24] A full defense for NDEs will be offered in Chapter 8.

## Conclusion

When I spoke of the reality that the human soul survived death and the evidence for NDEs defeating materialistic naturalism (that is, the idea that reality only relates to the physical world and rejects any notion of spiritual existence), she seemed to be a bit more relaxed when considering the

22. The experiences of NDEs and what can and cannot be learned from them will be explored in more detail in Chapter 8. For our purposes here, we want to illustrate the philosophical, theological, and scientific evidence that the human soul survives death in a disembodied state.

23. Habermas and Moreland, *Beyond Death*, 173.

24. At the time of publication, the Near-Death Experience Research Foundation (NDERF) reported more than 5,100 NDEs reported across the globe. See https://nderf.org.

prospect of death. Many members of her family had died, including one of her children. Sandy seemed a bit relieved to know that God designed human beings to live beyond the scope of this mere mortal existence. What are eighty or one hundred years in comparison to eternity? If all of life were merely found in the few years we live on this earth, life itself would be tragic. Sandy must have felt short-changed with the loss of her loved ones, seeing that she did not get a chance to have them in her life longer than she did.

However, our conversation had just begun. When I told her that the intermediate state was but the beginning of our journey and that we would be resurrected with new bodies, this brought about a further series of questions to her inquisitive mind. The questions regarding the location of the future heaven would be our next topic of conversation.

*Chapter Two*

_____

# WHERE IS HEAVEN
# LOCATED? (PART TWO)

*2 Corinthians 5:1–10 and Revelation 21:1–8*

1. *Will Be a Physical Location (21:1–2).*

2. *Will Be a Divine Location (21:3).*

3. *Will Be a Beautiful Location (21:4).*

4. *Will Be a National Location (21:5).*

S ANDY SEEMED TO ENJOY the description I gave concerning the disembodied spiritual existence we have after death. She appreciated the fact that when believers die, they enter God's presence. I noted that this is not the final picture of heaven. When Christ returns, he will resurrect the bodies of those who have died along with those who still live (1 Thess. 4:16–18). However, this brought up another question. Sandy asked, "If we are spiritual beings, why does God not just leave us that way instead of resurrecting us when he returns? What is the point of resurrection?"

Her question was not new. At a different church, one sweet church lady startled me with the revelation that she had never heard of the final resurrection. Aghast, I asked how this was possible seeing that the return of Christ and the final resurrection weigh so strongly in early Christian theology. She noted that no one had ever taught on the issue.

Returning to Sandy's question, I directed her to an ongoing theme throughout the entirety of Scripture. God is in the process of resurrecting all of creation to the place where he and his creation live in perfect harmony. In the previous chapter, we discussed the different perspectives relating to the spiritual state of existence once a person's physical body dies. We noted that the soul survival perspective is the only position that adheres to the teachings of Scripture, especially when considering Jesus's promise to the thief on the cross that he would experience paradise with Jesus on the day of his death. But as Paul asserted in 2 Corinthians, the spiritual state of existence is not the end of the story. A new state of existence comes when Jesus returns and resurrects the bodies of the saints. As we answer where heaven is located, it must be shown that heaven itself will transform when God recreates the cosmos. The heaven described in Revelation 21 has not arrived just yet. John notes that the new heaven and earth embody a state where the spiritual and physical are united and where God resides within creation with newfound unity. No sin will separate creation from God any longer.

Another theological question must be answered. Is this earth the place where heaven will be located? Or will God create a new cosmos when he establishes the new order? To answer this question, we must note that John acknowledges that the new heaven and new earth will replace the old heaven and earth as the "first heaven and the first earth had passed away" (Rev. 21:1). Another clue is given in Peter's second letter. Peter states that the "day of the Lord will come like a thief; on that day the heavens will pass away with a loud noise, the elements will burn and be dissolved, and the earth and the works on it will be disclosed" (2 Pet. 3:10).

I liken the new creation to a home that two of our family members built. Our cousins had purchased a nice house in the mountains of North Carolina. The home was an older house but served them well. They decided that they wanted to upgrade their home to something bigger and better than the house they had. So, they leveled the old house while maintaining its foundation. They built a new house that was much larger and far grander than the house they had previously held. God promises to do the same with the physical world. In Genesis, God noted that creation was good (Gen. 1:31). However, when he looks at the new creation, he may imitate Tony the Tiger, saying, "It's grrrreat!!!" More to the point, the new creation will be perfect. Everything good about this world will be perfected in the new creation.

Physical things are not evil. A good God created the physical world. I often love walking in the beauty of God's creation and considering its glory and grandeur. Creation's glory is glorious only because it comes from a glorious God. While we realize that the world is beautiful—and it truly is, it will not even come close to the beauty of the new creation. Revelation 21 describes four attributes of this new heavenly creation.

## Attribute #1: The Future Heaven will be a Physical Location (21:1–2)

John maintains that the new creation will be a physical location with a capital city. While it is physical, it is unlimited like the intermediate state. It may prove helpful to discuss a bit of biblical theology to help us understand. Going back to Genesis, sin infiltrated God's good creation resulting in a separation between God and humanity. Since God knew the fall would occur, he has been planning a restoration project even before the Garden. One word will help us at this juncture: *anastasis*. *Anastasis* is the Greek word for resurrection. The term is most often used for Jesus's resurrection (Luke 14:14) or the resurrection of the dead at the end of time (Acts 1:22).[1] Jesus says that he is the *anastasis* and the life (John 11:25). In a manner of speaking, the spirit of a person receives an *anastasis* of sorts as the believer is changed from a state of judgment into a state of grace (John 3:16–17). In like manner, one day believers will receive a physical *anastasis* when Christ returns (John 11:25; 14:3; and 1 Thess. 4:15–17). However, the physical body that is received at that time will be vastly different. The glorified body will be a spiritual body (1 Cor. 15:44). This spiritual body will maintain an aspect of physicality, but I believe it will be supercharged.

A former pastor of mine, the late Rev. Clate Brown, believed that with this new body, a person could think of a place and be transported there. While some may claim that this sounds too much like science fiction, remember that Jesus's resurrected body permitted him to do things that the normal body could not do. For instance, he could appear and disappear at will. Jesus disappeared from the two in Emmaus, but then somehow appeared in the middle of the Upper Room when the two arrived (Luke 24:30–43). Before you count this off as an apparition, remember that Jesus ate broiled fish with all in attendance (Luke 24:43). Comparable to the Star Trek beam, he was able to change his location without yelling for Scottie.

1. Mangun, *Lexham Theological Wordbook*.

18

This body is a supercharged spiritual/physical combination that will be unlike anything a person could imagine. If spiritual water were compared with gas and the physical with solid, then the resurrected body may be something comparable to plasma. Like plasma, the resurrected body may exist beyond the scope of simply the spiritual and physical, it may be a perfect combination of both.

When the Bible speaks of the new creation, it identifies this new creation as a resurrected place. It is a glorified physical place with all new laws of nature. Just as the new glorified body is super-charged, the new heaven and earth will be super-charged with amped and perfected physics. One difference is found in Revelation 21:23. In the text, John says that there is no longer a need for a sun or a moon to shine on the new creation because the "glory of God illuminates it" (Rev. 21:23). Does this indicate that there are no stars, planets, and galaxies? Not necessarily. It may merely suggest that the usefulness of the sun to lighten the Earth is no longer needed because God's radiance penetrates every aspect of this new creation. Even now, God's ontological presence is found in creation but not necessarily in his personal presence. In contrast, God's personal presence is found in every nook and cranny of the new creation.

Some hold that the New Jerusalem may be found elevated above the new earth. I am not sure of that, but I do know that the text shows an important truth that must be considered. The New Jerusalem is only part of the new creation. It is the capital city. But the new heaven and earth (Rev. 21:1) suggest that the universal structure will be transformed.

If you like exploring, you will love this new creation. All the beautiful scenes on earth will be intensified in this new creation. I have not had the opportunity to travel much in life. That is something that I would have wanted to have changed at this juncture in life. But with job changes, family responsibilities, and the busyness of life; I have never had a chance to explore the world as much as I would have wanted. However, this will change in the new creation. People will be able to discover sights even more spectacular than those found on earth.

We may possibly see more colors than we do now. Colors are what the eyes perceive as wavelengths from reflected light. However, the human eye can only see a small portion of the wavelengths that exist. Infrared and ultraviolet rays cannot be observed with the human eye. However, if you are as fair-skinned as I am, you will soon realize the existence of ultraviolet rays after standing outside in the sunlight for an extended period of time. One of the consistent reports from those experiencing NDEs is that heaven holds more colors than a person can see in this life. That stands to reason if you consider the limitless array of wavelengths detected by the spiritual eye. We should get excited about this new creation as it is going to be absolutely amazing!

## Attribute #2: The Future Heaven will be a Divine Location (21:3)

Next, the future heaven is noted to be a divine location. God speaks from heaven proclaiming that "God's dwelling is with humanity, and he will live with them. They will be his peoples, and God himself with be with them and will be their God" (Rev. 21:3). The curse from the Garden has been reversed! The separation between God and humanity is no more. This aspect is what makes heaven so heavenly. In the new creation, God permanently tabernacles with humanity. God essentially becomes our next-door neighbor. Can you imagine? This is remarkable considering the expanse that currently exists between the personal aspect of God and his people.

Paul, in his depiction of his NDE experience, held that the third heaven was the abode of God (2 Cor. 12:2). The number of heavens could extend beyond just three. According to Ludwig Blau and Kaufmann Kohler, the Talmud contends for the existence of seven heavens: 1. *Velon*—the sky (Isa. 49:22), 2. *Raki'a*—the universe, 3. *Shehakim*—where the millstones are to grind manna for the righteous (Ps. 78:23), 4. *Zebul*—the upper part of Zion where Michael offers his sacrifices (Isa. 63:15), 5. *Ma'on*—the location of the ministering angels (Deut. 26:15), 6. *Makon*—treasuries of universal materials (1 Kgs. 7:30), 7. *'Arabot*—the throne room of God.[2] While this interpretation cannot be proven, even if it were, five of the heavens would constitute what Paul termed the "third heaven." According to the pseudepigraphical work *The Apocalypse of Baruch,* Baruch, the scribe of Jeremiah, ascends through the five heavens. For the *Second Book of Enoch,* another Jewish pseudepigraphical book, the number is increased to ten heavens.[3] No matter the number of heavens, the new heaven and earth will

---

2. Blau and Kohler, "Angelology."

3. In 2 *Enoch*, the first heaven is noted to be the abode of the clouds and stars; the second heaven is the place of darkness, despair, and death; the third heaven is the mercy of paradise and the abode of hell; the fourth heaven is the location of the sun, moon, and stars; the fifth heaven is a place of silence, sadness, and regret; the sixth heaven is

eliminate any separation between God and humanity. God's children will be his people and God will be the people's God. Nothing will ever sever or separate the two.

I remember my godly mother once telling me, "If I go to heaven before you do, look for me at Jesus's feet, because that's where I plan to be." On another occasion, I visited a woman in hospice care. She told me with tears in her eyes, "Don't pray that I get better. Pray that I pass into eternity. I want to see Jesus." For both women, heaven constituted the place where Jesus was found. It was not about the glitz and glamour of heavenly sites. Rather, Jesus is what made heaven so wonderful. I think that should be true for every believer.

Since God permanently tabernacles with humanity in this place, the locale will be filled with God's divine characteristics. These attributes are best understood by the fruit of the Spirit (Gal. 5:22–23) which include love (*agape*), joy (*chara*), peace (*eirene*), patience (*makrothumia*), kindness (*chrestotes*), goodness (*agathosune*), faithfulness (*pistis*), gentleness (*prautes*), and self-control (*enkrateia*).

Imagine a time when someone showed you love. Maybe it was the caress of a mother or the passion of a lover's kiss. Imagine a time when you experienced great joy. Perhaps your mind goes back to some accomplishment you achieved or an experienced state of bliss. I think about the time that I defended my dissertation and felt the thrill and excitement of knowing that I could then be called a "doctor." Can you think of a time when you experienced peace—a moment when everything seemed right in the world? Do you recall a time when someone was patient with you? Maybe you have thoughts of a godly employer maintaining a calm demeanor as you tried to learn the job. Consider a time when someone was kind to you. Perhaps this includes a time when a charitable person gifted you with a present that you have never forgotten. Can you think of someone who was good to you? This person may have been someone you wished to emulate. What about faithfulness? Perhaps you recollected a spouse who remained faithful to you even when during your worst moments. Can you think of someone who has a gentle spirit, a person who would not even hurt a fly? Ponder a person

---

the place where the archangels and other angelic beings reside; the seventh heaven is the location of powers and dominions; the eight heaven controls the meteorological weather patterns on Earth; the ninth heaven consists of the celestial home of the stars of night; and the tenth heaven is home to the cherubim, seraphim, and the divine council of God. Remember, pseudepigraphal writings are not considered to be canonical.

you admire for their self-control. Maybe this person remained disciplined and a cool-headedness when everyone else was maddened.

Now that you have those pleasant thoughts in mind, realize that these are but foreshadows of the future heaven that awaits us. The love, joy, peace, patience, goodness, kindness, gentleness, faithfulness, and self-control that are encountered in this life pale in comparison to the perfection of these traits found in God. Heaven will be a place where the fruits of God's Spirit are experienced in a perfected form for all who enter therein.

Individuals will grow and grow in their relationship with the Lord. However, it must be noted that even our understanding of God's attributes is limited because we cannot understand perfect goodness. The late theologian Thomas Oden notes,

> When Christian teachers have cautiously applied that ordinary human word *good* to God, they have applied it analogically, that is, by some proportional comparison to what we know to be *like* human goodness, remaining aware that God's goodness is also vastly *unlike* human goodness (Gregory of Nyssa, *Ag. Eunomius* XI.1, 2, *NPNF* 2 V, pp. 230, 231; Bonaventure, *Soul's Journey into God*, *CWS*, VI, pp. 102 ff.) . . . Although God is insurmountably good, we know that even our best conceptions of goodness do not do full justice to the infinitely wise, eternal goodness of God.[4]

This leads me to believe that even in heaven God will not be fully understood. Heaven may be a place where believers spend an eternity learning and growing in the knowledge of the divine Creator of the cosmos. Each day in eternity may prove to provide additional insights into the ultimate good character of God. As good and wonderful as my professors have been, can you imagine what it will be like to have God as your eternal Professor?

## Attribute #3: The Future Heaven will be a Beautiful Location (21:4)

The third attribute of heaven is that of beauty. While other texts of Revelation depict the beauty of the golden street(s) and the vegetation found around the river of life, the aspect that grants heaven its true beauty is the death of death. Sandy had endured many physical ailments throughout her life. She wanted to know if heaven would be better. She is not the only one. Throughout my pastoral ministry and especially in chaplaincy ministry, I

4. Oden, *Living God*, 42.

have sat by the bedsides of many as they drew their last breath. On one occasion, I felt the spirit of a gentleman pass from his body into eternity as I laid my hand upon his shoulder as he passed. The presence and pain that death brings may have been what moved Jesus to tears before raising Lazarus back to life (John 11:35). In contrast, heaven will be a place with no tears, grief, crying, pain, and death. Because of Jesus's resurrection, death has died. The ultimate culmination of the death of death is found in the eternal life of heaven.

Can you imagine living without the fear of death? The fear of death impacts everything we do in life. We eat to keep from dying. We take medication to keep from dying. We do not get too close to the edge of the mountain for fear of falling to our deaths. We even work to pay the bills to have the essentials of life to keep from dying. Heaven is a place where people can live to their full potential without ever fearing death.

In one episode of the *Twilight Zone,* a Martian with three arms snuck into a café in hopes of upstarting a new Martian colony. When speaking with the owner of the café, he gave away his secret identity when the proprietor inquired why he was not wet after surviving a bus crash. The crash, unbeknownst to the café owner, was propagated by the alien. The Martian replied, "Wet. What is wet?" The café owner curiously asked, "What do you mean 'what is wet'?" It is then that the Martian revealed a third arm hidden by his trench coat, while acknowledging his intentions to colonize the planet Earth. All of this was done while puffing on a cigarette in classic 1960s fashion. The café owner then unveiled that he too was an alien. Pulling back his hat, the owner revealed a third eye and disclosed that he was a Venusian. He further noted that his friends from Venus intercepted and destroyed the Martian vessel, and they planned to colonize the planet with their kind instead.

Is it not interesting that the Martian did not understand the word *wet*? In the Twilight Zone adaptation, Martians did not know wet because they had no water to make them wet. Likewise, in heaven, the word *death* will not be in one's vocabulary. Why should it be? Death will no longer exist in heaven. That is what makes heaven so beautiful. Paul rightly says, "What no eye has seen, no ear has heard, and no human heart has conceived—God has prepared these things for those who love him" (1 Cor. 2:9).

## Attribute #4: The Future Creation will be a National Location (21:5–8)

Portions of this book were written at the close of one of the nastiest Presidential elections in recent history. The 2020 Presidential election divided families and friends over who was rightly elected as the 46th President of the United States. Friendships that had endured several years of comradery were ripped apart, sometimes at even the thought that a person would hold a different political conviction than one's own. The level of immaturity on social media only served as a microcosm of a culture deprived of respect and humility.

In contrast to the political madness of recent years, the fourth attribute of heaven notes the integrity of the political and national traits of the kingdom of God. No matter where you are reading this book, understand that your nation will not survive into eternity. Only one kingdom will remain—the Kingdom of God. We will have more to say about the kingdom in a later chapter. For now, consider the ruler of this heavenly land. John describes the political ruler of this place as the Triune God (21:5). Father, Son, and Holy Spirit will rule and reign for all eternity. No more political parties! No more political debates. Praise God, no more political campaign ads. The Lamb will prove victorious over the elephant, donkey, and any other political animals added to the zoo.

This ruler gives freely of his grace to anyone thirsty, he does not withhold from anyone their need (21:6). God's grace will not be withheld from his citizens. He has made everything new. Notice in verse 6, God says to John, "It is done" (21:6)! When Jesus died on the cross, he said, "*tetelestai*"—i.e., "it is finished" (John 19:30). *Tetelestai* depicts bringing a previous act to a close. Now, the Lamb says, "*ginomai*"—i.e., "it is done" (21:6). *Ginomai* indicates something that happens which brings about a new state from the one previously experienced.[5] The government would be completely new. The heavenly government will be perfect, with a perfect ruler, and perfected citizens (21:7–8). As Thomas Oden notes, it will be a place with "no more homelessness."[6]

While the church is saved, believers still have trouble relating to one another. Churches are constantly rifled with divisions and split over committees and constitutions. A friend of mine told me of a church in the

---

5. Louw and Nida, *Greek-English Lexicon of the NT*, 13.107, 160.

6. Oden, *Life in the Spirit*, 2:462.

Appalachian Mountains of North Carolina that split over toilet paper. Yes, you read that correctly. Toilet paper. No, I am not kidding. The story goes, some members complained that the custodian was not doing a sufficient job. When the custodian changed the toilet paper from one brand to another (I believe she changed it from Charmin to Angel Soft), the church split. Yes, the church split over toilet paper. With that being the case, there is no wonder why the church went down the toilet. The members flushed their mission down the drain. Okay, okay. I'll stop. Hmm . . . but I do wonder if they will sit on their thrones in heaven? Alright. Seriously. I'm done now. In heaven, Christians will finally relate to one another with the love and compassion that God intended for them to have. The church will finally be the church in this new kingdom. For the church previously noted, the stain of their tainted toilet paper will be eradicated. I promise that is the last reference.

## Conclusion

Ministry has not been easy for me. Ministerial battles have often left me tattered and torn. Once, I was so distraught, I thought about exiting all ministry completely. Even after returning to ministry, I had thought I could not continue any longer. As I lay in bed, the Spirit of God came upon me. The Holy Spirit ministered by granting me a time of joyful bliss and perfect peace only because of his presence. I almost felt as if I were floating in my bed because of the Spirit's amazing anointing that evening. I have often thought about that experience. I wish the Spirit of God continued to come over me as he did that evening. However, I realize now that the joy that the encounter brought was only a foretaste of the heavenly pleasures awaiting us in God's kingdom.

Death is understandably scary for anyone as one enters a new state of being. But the good news is that the believer must only die once. Famed pastor and revivalist Jonathan Edwards emphasized the importance of holding an eternal perspective. An eternal perspective helps us through uncertain days. As Bob Dill of Huntsville Baptist Church once said, "Understanding biblical prophecy, we know that things will get bad, and then they will get worse for the believer. But eventually, things will get better and better." This is a perspective I shared with Sandy. She seemed to be encouraged by the biblical eschatological portrayal, understanding that when a believer dies, he or she spiritually enters God's presence, but that eventually all of creation will be resurrected into a glorious new creation. Even though this information was wonderful to her ears, Sandy was a woman who kept herself together. She realized her body was failing her. She wanted to know about the bodily state she would hold in this new creation. For the answer, we must move to her next question.

# Chapter Three

## WHAT WILL OUR BODIES BE LIKE IN HEAVEN?

*1 Corinthians 15:35–49*

1. Analogies of the Resurrected Body (1 Cor. 15:35–41).

    a. *Analogous to the Survival of a Harvested Seed (15:35–38)*

    b. *Analogous to the Superiority of the Human Species (15:39)*

    c. *Analogous to the Splendor of the Heavenly Stars (15:40–41)*

2. Attributes of the Resurrected Body (1 Cor. 15:42–49)

    a. *The Imperishable Attribute (15:42, 45a, 47a)*

    b. *The Glorified Attribute (15:43a, 49)*

    c. *The Powerful Attribute (15:43b)*

    d. *The Spiritual Attribute (15:44, 46, 48)*

    e. *The Heavenly Attribute (15:47b)*

U P TO THIS POINT, I had been pacing in front of the altar of the church with excitement to speak on these issues. For those who are theological nerds like me, it is not often that one gets to engage in such deep conversations. However, by this point in the conversation, my ankles notified me that my pacing needed to halt by their burning throbbing. They had sustained many years walking on the concrete floor of an industrial complex and suffered the impact of jumping on and off machinery. Needing to get off my feet, I nestled into the front pew of the church. Reclining on the pew with my legs propped up on the comfortable green cushion beneath and my arm propped on the rustic wooden frame on top, I was then ready to continue my conversation with Sandy.

Sandy was a woman who took always donned a neat appearance. She was not one to "beat around the bush." If she liked you, then you had earned a lifelong friend. If she did not, then it was best to leave her alone. Laziness was a trait that grated her nerves. Why? Laziness and slothfulness bothered her because she worked hard her entire life. Everything she owned came from hard work. She cared for her family the best she could and went above and beyond to ensure that their needs were met. Thus, when her body was unable to perform the tasks she desired, she was left irritated and troubled.

Sandy continued our conversation by saying, "I recall preachers talking about Jesus coming back to get his church. This is an issue that does not make sense to me. If our souls go to heaven when we die, then why does Jesus need to come back to get us? If it is true that our spirits go to be with Jesus, we are already with him. Why does he need to come to get us if we are already there?"

Often in church life, principles and truths are given without considering the ramifications of what is said. Before speaking with Sandy, I had not considered how this may leave people confused. Sandy brought up a great point. Jesus said that he would come to get us and take us to where he was (John 14:1–4). But if we are already there with him, why is such a task needed? Sandy referenced the *Parousia* of the church. Paul, most likely citing an early Christian creed, notes the following:

> We who are still alive at the Lord's coming will certainly not precede those who have fallen asleep. For the Lord himself will descend from heaven with a shout, with the archangel's voice, and the trumpet of God, and the dead in Christ will rise first, then we who are still alive, who are left, will be caught up together with them in the clouds to meet the Lord in the air, and so we will always be with the Lord (1 Thess. 4:11).

Jesus's second coming is a doctrine that was held by the earliest church and resonates throughout the teachings of the NT. But how does the spiritual existence of the person in heaven negate the need for such an appearance?

Directing Sandy to 2 Corinthians 5, the concept of the continued spiritual state in heaven is not shown to be the final state. Paul teaches that the spirit of the believer groans to have one's heavenly dwelling (2 Cor. 5:2). However, the spiritual state in heaven is likened to a form of nakedness (2 Cor. 5:3). The believer will find one's home in the completely transformed being in the resurrected body. Believers, Paul exhorts, should seek to please Christ in whatever form in which one is found—the current physical body, the spiritual body, or the glorified body. To recap, the current holistic person will be transformed. First, the spirit is saved and transformed (John 3:16). Second, the spirit leaves the body at death to be enjoined with God in one's heavenly home (2 Cor. 5:8). Finally, Christ will return at the Father's command accompanied by the angel's trumpet blast to resurrect the church with glorified, resurrected bodies. Believers will follow the model set forth by Christ. Christ's spirit departed his body at his death. When his spirit returned, he was resurrected with a glorified body. When Christ returns, the believer will encounter their own Easter experience. No matter if the body is nothing more than a few specks of dust, Christ will resurrect the body and grant a new spiritual/physical glorified body. God changes a person holistically—body, soul, and spirit will all be resurrected by Christ. The spiritual heaven is only part of the equation. The other part of the equation is found with the glorified body.

Sandy was amazed at this teaching. She asked, "What will this glorified body be like?" Her last question serves as the basis of this chapter. Like Sandy, I have also known what physical decline is like. When I was in my early 30s, I hit amazing numbers in the gym. I squatted more than 800 lbs. and bench pressed over 500 lbs. at one juncture. When digestive issues placed me in the Emergency Room on three separate occasions, my strength levels suffered. Admittedly, I cannot wait to test-drive the glorified body. To attempt to understand the glorified body, Sandy and I discussed the resurrection chapter found in 1 Corinthians 15.

A story is told of a young child complaining to her mother that her stomach hurt. "Oh, honey, your stomach is empty," the mother responded. "You just need to get something in it, and you'll be fine." About a week later, the pastor was ailing and speaking with her mother that he had a headache. Being as quick-witted as she was, the little girl said, "Oh, pastor, my mommy says that your head is empty. You just need to get something in it, and you'll be fine."[1] Hopefully, our minds will be full by the time we attempt to understand the glorified body.

In what is classically known as the resurrection chapter, Paul discusses the essentials of Christ's resurrection, even giving one of the most ancient pre–New Testament texts (15:3–8). He then describes the essential nature of the resurrection to our faith (15:12–19) before noting the guarantee of our resurrection bodies from Christ's resurrection (15:20–28). Additionally, Paul ensures the support of the resurrection from the Christian experience (15:29–34). In verses 35–49, Paul then directs his attention to the nature of the resurrection body itself. What will our resurrection bodies be like? Paul answers this question by two means. First, he describes the glorified body using analogies. Second, Paul uses more concrete language meriting the attributes of the glorified body.

## Analogies of the Resurrected Body (1 Cor. 15:35–41)

Some of the Corinthians thought that the resurrected body would be the same as the present body. What a miserable hope they had! Paul corrects their thinking by using three analogies to describe the differences between the resurrected body and the current physical body. Analogies, while often imperfect, provide general insight as to what one can expect with a future pending event. The differences are quite remarkable.

### Analogous to the Survival of a Harvested Seed (15:35–38)

First, Paul uses the analogy of a harvested seed to note the survival of the glorified body. Paul uses the analogy of a seed. The seed is placed in the ground as if it were dead. Once in the ground, the seed develops into new life. The body that dies and is sown in the ground is to be raised back to life in a new form. Did Paul believe that the seed died? Some commentators argue over Paul's use of the term *apothnēskō* when relating to the concept of dying. Did Paul believe that the seed died when it is planted in the ground or was his use of the term for death merely symbolic? Quite frankly, it does not matter. He is using an analogy to bring out a greater spiritual point.

While Paul is unconcerned with the precise scientific aspects of agricultural planting, he is concerned with a twofold inquiry: first, the manner

1. Hodgin, *1001 Humorous Illustrations for Public Speaking*, 194–95.

of the resurrection, and second, the future state of the quality of the resurrected body.[2] The manner of the resurrection follows a similar pattern to the seed that is sewn. Like the seed planted in the earth, the body dies and is planted in the ground. Similar to the seed that produces new life, so also the body will give way to a new form of life. Death must first occur to give way to a glorious new life.

The future state of the glorified body flows from the first question. The more educated among the Corinthians would have considered resurrection reprehensible. Ramsay MacMullen notes that "Resurrection in the flesh appeared a startling, distasteful idea, at odds with everything that passed for wisdom among the educated."[3] They inquired, if the body decomposes and is disintegrated into other life forms (i.e., plants, animals, etc.), then how could the body be resurrected in a similar form? Modern objectors could ask, is the resurrected body something akin to Frankenstein with patches from different persons comprising his final form? What a horrid idea, indeed! Paul notes that the glorified body holds both continuity and discontinuity with the body of the old.[4] The glorified body will hold similar traits to the old body, especially regarding the look of the face and structure.[5] While there is some continuity between the old body and the glorified body, Paul also argues that there is an aspect of discontinuity which will be in view when he discusses the attributes of the glorified body as noted later in the chapter.

My grandmother, Eva Chilton, was a wonderful, godly lady. She loved all kinds of trees and flowers. She planted several silver maple trees in front of her house and a couple in front of my old childhood home. She planted the maple as a seed. Before long, the silver maple, known for being a fast-growing deciduous tree, aligned her house with shade. While she and my grandpa Roy never owned an air-conditioner, the shade from the trees in addition to their window-unit fans provided the necessary coolness to keep them comfortable in the hot and humid summer months of northwestern North Carolina. Her small handful of silver maple seeds developed into the silver maple trees that provided oxygen and a haven of rest for birds and

2. Wright, *Resurrection of the Son of God,* 343.

3. MacMullen, *Christianizing the Roman Empire,* 12.

4. Ciampa and Rosner, *First Letter to the Corinthians,* 800.

5. This will prove helpful in chapter six when discussing the aspect of knowing other people in heaven. Our faces will be recognized as they will be similar to the faces we now have. Note that the disciples knew Jesus of Nazareth after his resurrection because of the continuity that was held from the old body and the glorified body.

local squirrels. Later, the trees would serve as markers for pick-up games of football for us during summertime get-togethers. The point is that the trees became something distinct from the seeds originally planted. They stemmed from the seeds, but their form was far different and much grander.

One could also use Paul's analogy to compare the body to that of a butterfly. The caterpillar seemingly dies when it wraps itself in a cocoon. However, when it resurfaces, the wiggling creature has now become a soaring butterfly that can fly to new heights that its former form never could.

As I write this, I find myself mourning the loss of a good friend and another member of Huntsville Baptist Church. Lisa Jester was a woman who was full of life. She suffered from many health conditions throughout her life. After having major surgery, she would eventually succumb to complications that emerged from the procedure. Writing this section has proved somewhat therapeutic for me as I recount the change that Lisa will experience at the resurrection. With her glorified body, Lisa will never suffer from any ailments she suffered on Earth. The reality is that we all must experience death. But the promise in Christ is that the body that Christ gives us at his Second Coming will be unlike anything we could ever imagine.

## Analogous to the Superiority of the Human Species (15:39)

Next, Paul compares the species of the human race to the animal kingdom. Just as the human being is superior to animals in their rational and spiritual capacity, so will the glorified body be superior to the current form of the body. As Paul says, "Not all flesh is the same flesh" (15:39). Just as various bodies exist, the skeptical Corinthian should not assume that the glorified body and the old body are the same. If God can create the vast panoply of bodies in the current world, why then should one deny the possibility that God could create something even greater in the resurrected body? If God is the greatest Being that could ever be conceived, then the perfected body promised to believers will be the greatest body that could ever be conceived. As we noted previously in the book, there are good reasons for holding to the spiritual cohabitation of the departed soul with God's presence in paradise after one's death. Yet that is not the final promised state. The glorified body will be the best of possible bodies that the human being could ever hold.

## Analogous to the Splendor of the Heavenly Stars (15:40–41)

Third, Paul affords an analogy of the body with the splendor of heavenly stars and planetary bodies. Ciampa and Rosner contend that Paul had in mind the creation narrative. Verses 36–38 relate the seed-bearing plants and animals to Genesis 1:11–13 with Day Three of the creation story; verse 39a relates humans to Genesis 1:26–28 of Day Six of creation; verse 39b relates animals to Genesis 1:24–25 of Day Six of creation; verse 39c relates birds to Genesis 1:20b, 21b of Day Five of creation; and verses 40–41 relate the heavenly lights to Genesis 1:14–19 of Day Four of the creation story.[6] The heavenly bodies of verses 40–41 depict astronomical objects and not celestial beings as some have held.[7] The word *splendor* in the CSB and *glory* in the NKJV is the term *doxa* in Greek. *Doxa* describes the splendor or magnificence of a thing.

As the apostle depicts, the sun has a greater splendor than the moon. When a lunar eclipse takes place, the moon moves into the earth's shadow. A person can view the eclipse with the naked eye because the eye is not endangered by the moon's light. However, when a solar eclipse happens, such is not the case. A solar eclipse occurs when the moon is aligned in such a way that it blocks the rays of the sun from a portion of the earth. Many readers will remember the great Solar Eclipse of 2017. My family gathered during the eclipse and watched the phenomenon with specially coated sunglasses which allowed us to watch the solar eclipse without frying our eyes. The ultraviolet rays from the sun wreak havoc upon the eyes when viewing the sun unaided, even during an eclipse.[8] The splendor of the sun's rays is more glorious than the reflective light of the moon. However, other stars are more splendorous than even our sun.

Paul's use of the glories of different stars is on target with what one finds in the illustrious foray of celestial objects in the night sky. The sun finds itself in the lower middle of a wide-ranging spectrum of celestial stars. Stars are classified by the letters O, B, A, F, G, K, and M. The classifications can be remembered by the funny saying, "Oh, Be A Fine Girl/Guy, Kiss Me."

6. Ciampa and Rosner, *First Letter to the Corinthians*, 805.

7. Wright explains, "If Paul is aware of a shift in meaning between 'heavenly' as meaning 'the location of the sun, moon and stars,' as is in the present passage, and 'heavenly' as he uses it in verses 48–49, he does not indicate it, but leaves his readers to make the transition through his move . . . from metaphor and simile to explicit description." Wright, *Resurrection of the Son of God*, 346.

8. The only exception is for the few seconds when a total eclipse occurs.

Spectral O-type stars are the brightest and hottest stars. O-type stars are blue supergiants. They are comprised of ionized helium and range from a temperature of 49,940 to 89,540 degrees Fahrenheit. B-type stars are blue-white stars that contain helium and some hydrogen and range from 17,540 to 49,940 degrees Fahrenheit.

A-type stars are white stars that contain strong hydrogen and some ionized metals. A-type stars range from 13,040 to 17,540 degrees Fahrenheit. F-type stars are white stars. They contain both hydrogen and ionized metals such as calcium and iron. Their temperature ranges from 10,340 to 13,040 degrees Fahrenheit.

Our sun is classified as a G-type star. G-type stars are yellow stars ranging from 8,540 to 10,340 degrees Fahrenheit. These stars are made of both metals and ionized metals, helium, hydrogen, and ionized calcium.

K-type stars are orange stars that range from 5,840 to 8,540 degrees Fahrenheit and are made of metals. Finally, M-type stars are red stars that range from 4,040 to 5,840 degrees Fahrenheit and are made of titanium oxide, calcium, and other elements. Truly, Paul was correct in that different stars hold various levels of luminosity and/or glory.

Going back to the sun's comparison to other stars, consider how the sun compares to O-type stars. For instance, the sun's radius is around 432,376 miles across with a surface temperature of approximately 10,000 degrees Fahrenheit. Compare the sun's dimensions with VY Canis Majoris, the largest known star in the universe at the time of publication. It has a radius of 613.67 million miles. This massive star has a surface temperature of 4,940 degrees Fahrenheit, nearly half as much as the sun's temperature. VY Canis Majoris is a red supergiant and spectral K-type star, whereas the Sun is a G-type main-sequence star, often called a yellow dwarf.

As previously noted, the hottest stars in the cosmos are the O-type blue supergiants. They are rarer than the red dwarf stars, the coolest stars in the night sky. One of the hottest known stars in the universe is WR 102 which boasts an estimated surface temperature of 377,540 degrees Fahrenheit. That is over 37 times hotter than the sun! MACS J1149, or "Icarus" (B-type); Rigel (B-type); UW Canis Majoris (O-type); and Zeta Puppis (O-type) are also considered blue supergiants.

Leaving our astronomical observations and going back to Paul's perspective—just as different stars display varying degrees of splendor; the glorified body is far more splendid than the present body. The moon cannot compare to the rays of the sun. It certainly cannot compare to the rays of WR 102, UW Canis Majoris, or the other blue supergiants. Similarly, the present body is comparable to the moon, whereas the glorified body is comparable to a blue supergiant. Unlike the blue supergiant, the glorified body will not quickly burn out of its fuel. The splendor and glory far surpass anything that we could imagine. The body will be similar in its appearance, but its splendor will be greatly magnified. This brings us to the second question that Paul posed in the resurrection chapter. What are the areas of discontinuity between the old body and the glorified body?

## Attributes of the Resurrected Body (1 Cor. 15:42–49)

As noted earlier in the chapter, Paul describes both the continuity of the old body with the glorified body as seen in similar faces and bodily structures. However, in verses 42–49, Paul notes the discontinuity that is found between the old body and the new. The glorified body possesses attributes that the old one does not hold. The apostle affords five such characteristics noting that the resurrected body is imperishable, glorified, powerful, spiritual, and heavenly.

### The Imperishable Attribute (15:42, 45)

First, Paul teaches in verse 42 that while the present body is sown in corruption—*phthora* which means literally *to rot;* it is a body that will corrode and die—the resurrected body will be imperishable. The word for "imperishable" is *aphtharsia* meaning that which is incapable of rotting. Paul's terminology indicates that the resurrected body will never age, disease, or die. The imperishable body is alive for all eternity. It is the epitome of perfect health.

In verse 45, Paul notes that as the first Adam (representing the historical Adam) became a living being, the "last Adam" (15:45), meaning Christ, became a "life-giving spirit" (15:45). Christ provides this resurrected body by way of his resurrection. Christ's resurrection and resurrected body are a forerunner to the kind that people will experience when he returns.

People have often erroneously claimed that the resurrection of Jesus is like the resuscitation of other people who have returned from death. This is most certainly not the case. Jesus's resurrection brought about a transformation in his human body. The difference is that those who return to life will die again. Jesus's resurrection is a complete reversal. The resurrected body will live forever.

Previously, we noted the wonder that will come in the hereafter with a life void of the fear of death. This fear limits our experiences. For instance, I am a very poor swimmer. I have often wished that I could observe the underwater wonders of the ocean. However, that cannot happen because of my inability to swim. The fear of drowning keeps me from going into deep water. But what if my body lost its ability to die? What if my body no longer required oxygen to live? If such were the case, then nothing could stop me from diving into the deep end of the pool or standing at the edge of a cliff. Life gains an entirely new dimension with an imperishable body.

## The Glorified Attribute (15:43a, 49)

Second, Paul holds that the resurrected body is dissimilar to the previous one because of the glorified attribute. The natural body is said to be sown in "dishonor" (15:43a). *Dishonor* is translated from the term *atimia* which means to be in a state of dishonor or disrespect. In contrast, *doxa* describes the resurrected body as it is clothed with the glory of God.

Concerning verse 43, Paul also noted that the resurrection body will bear the image of the "man of heaven," referring to Christ. The current body is infected with sinful inclinations. While we are redeemed by the grace of God, we cannot live perfect lives. We have been justified by the grace of God, meaning that we have been made right in the eyes of God. Believers experience the process of sanctification by which they are made into the likeness of Christ. In heaven and with our new physical resurrected bodies, we will be glorified, meaning that we will be perfected like Christ. We will be able to relate to each other in a fresh new way where we will not hurt each other as often happens in this present life. We will not sin because of our perfected inclinations and desires.

Sandy did not feel like she fit in with certain Christian groups because of the past hurt she had experienced at the hands of other believers. She was not alone. I have been hurt numerous times in ministry. I have often asked myself, "Why do I keep putting myself in these circumstances?" Or "Why does God keep putting me in circumstances where either I or my family get hurt?" Those who have left the church note that they do not want to attend church with all the so-called hypocrites.

But Paul offers the answer to these problems. The Church is not perfected yet. Because of our lack of perfection, we find that we are all hypocrites to a degree as we all have insufficiencies and hold the potential to misunderstand and be misunderstood. Some people fear being left out of certain functions and activities, so they will overload themselves to keep from FOMO—the fear of missing out. Others do not want to be overloaded with activities and do not care if they miss out on certain activities. When taking an abnormal psychology class, one truth became resolutely clear— everyone is abnormal to a degree. The key question is whether the person's abnormality keeps him or her from functioning in the real world. Because of all these challenges, no one can live up to the standards of God. Yet when the resurrected body is given, then the Church will be perfected because each person's body, mind, and soul will be perfected. Not only will people be able to relate to God as he deserves, but believers will also be able to relate to other believers the way they should. Emotional as well as physical problems will be healed and resolved.

## The Powerful Attribute (15:43b)

Third, Paul describes the resurrected body as powerful. The present body is weak as it will decay and die. However, the resurrected body is raised in power. The term *dunamis* indicates the potential to exert force. The resurrected body will exert far more force than the present body ever could. When a person engages in weightlifting, the muscle is torn down to rebuild itself stronger. Over time, the body's ability to recuperate fades. The horrible aspect of weightlifting is that if a person gets sick and cannot lift for a while, then the body weakens and loses the gains previously acquired. The weightlifter then loses all the gains they had struggled to accomplish. In contrast, the resurrected body will increasingly gain its ability to lift and run exponentially. The resurrected body is raised in power and is immortal. The body loses the ability to die. With this in mind, the body does not weaken over time. Instead, it only grows stronger.

The potential abilities only dreamed about by writers of the Marvel and DC comics will be actualized in the promised resurrected body. The band AC/DC performed the song "Highway to Hell." Their song illustrates the mindset that hell will be a fun place where boundaries and restrictions are eliminated. However, contemplation of Scripture reveals the opposite to be true. In heaven, with this resurrected body, the possibilities are endless! As an avid weightlifter, I must confess that I cannot wait to test drive the promised glorified body. The resurrected body requires no wheelchairs, prescription medication, or physicals. Can you imagine playing football and baseball with this new body? I may even be able to play basketball with this new body, a game that has not fared well for me with this old body. Being short and stiff does not help one's chances of doing well in a game geared for tall and fast people. Nonetheless, those things that people would like to do but cannot with this body are possible with the new one. The resurrected body is the greatest body that one could ever conceive because it is the promised hope by God, the greatest Being that one could ever conceive.

## The Spiritual Attribute (15:44–46, 48)

Fourth, Paul describes the resurrected body as a spiritual body. In verse 44, Paul notes that the body is sown as a physical body but is raised as a spiritual body. Paul again describes the process in verse 46. The physical body comes first, then death, and finally, the spiritual body is raised. The physical body is linked with the "man of dust" (15:48), that is, Adam. The spiritual body is aligned with the "man of heaven" (15:48), that is, Christ.

What is a *spiritual body*? *Pneumatikos sōma* is the phrase used for the spiritual body in Greek. The term *pneumatikos* indicates a metaphysical entity, one that is neither material nor physical.[9] Yet *sōma* indicates something that is physical.[10] Literally, the glorified body will be an immaterial material body.

Some scholars have claimed that the going thought of Paul's day was that the soul was made of lighter physical stuff.[11] Thus, the spirit was physical, just not the same weight as the body. However, this concept is difficult to accept. If the spirit (*ruach*) of humanity is considered of the lighter physical variety, would the Holy Spirit (*ruach ha kodesh*) not also be held to be a physical entity? Would this not also make God a physical Being rather than the immaterial God? While some accept this rigid monism, a literal rendering of Scripture tends to provide the duality of humanity. This does not mean that dualism should be stretched too far. The end goal is a holistic transformation of mind, body, and soul. However, accepting a strict biblical monistic[12] concept requires a few hermeneutical gymnastics that extends

---

9. Louw-Nida, *Greek-English Lexicon of the NT,* 79.3, 693.

10. Louw-Nida, *Greek-English Lexicon of the NT,* 9.8, 104.

11. Martin, *Corinthian Body,* 126–29.

12. As a reminder, monism is the belief that only the physical body exists and not an immaterial soul.

beyond the scope of Scripture. At best, monism ignores or manipulates, at worst, the term *pneumatikos.*

If monism is not the answer, can one say that the body is strictly spiritual and not physical? This commits the same fallacy as the previous position. To claim that the spiritual body is strictly spiritual and not somewhat physical is to deny the second descriptor—*sōma.* Thus, this Gnostic idea that the spiritual essence is better than the physical creation does not find a home in a biblical worldview. Yes, there is an eternal essence of humanity found in the spirit. But this is not to say that the physical world holds no value. How does one tread this conundrum?

A holistic theory of the spiritual body appears to work best. The spiritual body is a *psychosomatic* body infusing both spirit and flesh into a perfect entity that can tread in both physical and spiritual realms.[13] As Thomas Oden notes, "The *soma pneumatikon* is a body existing in continuity with our present body but one that does not inherit corruption (1 Cor. 15:50–53). The spiritual body does not lack a body, but is embodied in a glorified manner."[14] People now exist as a body housing a spirit. We are limited in what we can do with our bodies. But the glorified psychosomatic body is a spirit housing a body. It finds itself with no limitations and with a perfected moral character. The psychosomatic body is spiritually directed and full of the Holy Spirit.

Jesus gives us a foretaste of the powers that a psychosomatic body holds. For instance, Jesus ate fish but disappeared and reappeared at a moment's notice (Luke 24:35–43). Ah! Think of all the practical jokes that we could pull. When my mother worked as a third-shift nurse, I used to prank her. She would come home while I was hiding behind a chair. I would jump out and scare her. The laugh was on me when she faked an ailment after one of my pranks. She could have won an academy award for her performance. This proved to be the last time I would try something like that with my mom. Nonetheless, the body that Jesus had is the firstfruits of the body that we will have.

The glorified psychosomatic body can journey in both the spiritual and physical realms. This was the original intention of God in the Garden of Eden. The Garden of Eden was almost like a portal between heaven and

---

13. The term "psychosomatic" is not to be confused with the medical condition by the same name. Here, "psychosomatic" is used to describe the spiritually empowered glorified body.

14. Oden, *Word of Life,* 481.

earth. It was a place where God communed personally with humans, beings created to be the caretakers of Earth. Michael Heiser intriguingly notes that the original task of humanity was "to make the entire Earth like Eden."[15] Later, the temple complex became a portal where God met humanity—a portal between the spiritual and physical. Humanity was able to commune with God while in a physical body. This spiritual body, the glorified psychosomatic body, will be able to do just that, except that it will be able to tread where angels trod without visionary experiences. This body will exist in perfect harmony in both heaven and Earth. Thus, the glorified body will be the best possible body that a person could have.

## The Heavenly Attribute (15:47b)

The fifth and final descriptor Paul gives of this new glorified body is that it is a heavenly one. Paul says that the resurrected body is "from heaven" (15:47). The fifth attribute further helps us clarify what Paul meant by the "spiritual body." The body that Adam possesses is the same body that we now possess. It is a natural body. The natural body is made for Earth. It is not designed to tread the hallways of heaven. Thus, the natural body returns to the dust from which it is made. However, the spiritual body is built for heaven. It is a human body 2.0. This heavenly body is a super-charged, turbo, high-velocity, high-impact, strong, agile, perfected, energized, incredible, and rejuvenating body, unlike anything that has ever been witnessed. The heavenly body is built for intergalactic, interdimensional travel. The heavenly body is fine-tuned for eternal life in heaven. This physical body cannot see God in his full glory. However, the heavenly body will. Heavenly bodies are tuned in to their heavenly citizenship.

When I took collegiate electrical classes in an industrial maintenance program, I joined a tour group that ventured into one of the local hydro-electric power plants. We examined the generators and were amazed by the massive turbines. There was an area on the second floor that we could not explore. A cage door blocked us from entering the flash protection zone. The sign to the right of the door read, "Warning: Electric Arc flash hazard. Will cause severe injury or death." The sign noted that the electrical voltage was so strong and unstable coming off the generators that it would easily arc and hit anything, or anyone, standing nearby. The only way to access the area was to have specialized personal protective equipment (PPE) built to withstand

15. Heiser, *Unseen Realm*, 51.

the electrical charge of something comparable to 14,000 volts. More than 50 volts and a current of 0.1 to 0.2 amperes are considered lethal.[16]

The Bible states that no one can stand in the presence of God in one's current bodily form. Moses wanted to see God. However, Yahweh warned him that "You cannot see my face, for humans cannot see me and live" (Exod. 33:20). Therefore, Yahweh walked by Moses and covered his face until he had passed by. Then, he removed his hand and allowed Moses to see his back. Other passages denote the impossibility of a person seeing God in his full glory (John 1:18; 6:46; 1 Tim. 1:16–17).[17] Likely, a person is not allowed to see God for their protection. Quite possibly, a person would vaporize in their current form when seeing the majesty and awesome power of the Almighty. Yet with the heavenly body, God will dwell among his people, and his people will dwell with him (Rev. 21:1–5). Our heavenly bodies will allow us access to see God in all of his glory and power. This body will be the greatest body that one could ever conceive. It will gaze upon the Being than which nothing greater could be conceived, as it exists in a place that is greater than anything that could be conceived.

## Conclusion

As Sandy and I finished speaking about the resurrected body, I noticed a twinge of excitement in her voice. This hard-working lady found great excitement in the promised hope of a better body. She realized that her body was failing her. Her body simply could not keep up with her spirit. She desired to do so much that her body no longer permitted.

---

16. Voltage is the potential difference between two poles of electricity and measured in volts. The larger the difference between the negative and positive poles, the more voltage one holds. The current of electricity measured in amperes is the flow of electricity. Often, high voltages do not produce high amps. But the blast from a high voltage contact could cause serious or lethal damage.

17. At other times, it appears that people did have encounters with God where they saw him face to face (Gen. 32:30; Judg. 13; Isa. 6:1). With the exception of Isaiah, individuals saw the embodied form of Yahweh. For Isaiah, his encounter may be described as seeing a portion of God's glory but not his full essence. Or perhaps Isaiah had an out-of-body experience where he was able to see God in some form. Going back to the case of Moses's encounter with God, John J. Davis is probably right in his assessment, noting that "What really occurred on Mount Sinai between Moses and God on this occasion will never be fully known. Undoubtedly Moses saw things which the human tongue would be incapable of uttering." Davis, *Moses and the Gods*, 305.

As an amateur astronomer, I would like to visit many places in the cosmos that I simply cannot with this present body of flesh. We can see the rings of Saturn and the Great Red Storm of Jupiter, but we cannot see them up close or even touch them. It is said that Triton, one of Jupiter's moons, possesses volcanoes that spew out blue liquid nitrogen. Instead of burning a person on touch, this volcanic lava would freeze a person on contact. Imagine visiting Triton without the fear of freezing or burning. The universe holds so many places to observe and see that we simply cannot visit with these bodies. It is sad, really. Yet the new glorified body will not be so restrained.

Hopefully, this chapter has brought about visions of what this new body will be like. As I wrote this chapter, I spoke with Leo Percer and some others online. Together, we envisioned the amazing trips that we might take. We even made pacts to travel the universe together when we receive this new glorified body. Some may snark, "Ah, you're just imagining things!" That which is retorted as a dreadful thing is becoming a grave problem for some branches of modern Christianity. Many keep saying what heaven cannot be to the point that most have lost the vision of what heaven could be.

Sandy had been plagued by holier-than-thou types who only envisioned heaven as one long church service. She dreaded a place that she should have anticipated because others had dampened the possibilities of heaven with their own myopic vision. These people were not bad. None of them intended to cause any harm. However, their problem was that their vision of heaven was too small. Will there be times of worship in heaven? Of course! Will worship services encompass all there is to heaven? Of course not! Heaven is far greater than your wildest imagination. The body you will receive will be far greater than anything you can ever imagine. While many things in life do not live up to their expectations, the resurrected body will be far more glorious than you could ever dream. Dream your wildest dreams about the resurrected body. The things only envisioned in Marvel comics and science fiction will become reality in heaven. No, we may not turn green and become monsters. But we may very well have the strength of twelve Hulks.

Furthermore, dream your wildest dreams about heaven because death will be forever removed. Death loses its sting when we dream our wildest dreams about heaven. Donald Grey Barnhouse, whose first wife died, was driving his kids from the funeral. One of the kids said, "Daddy, I don't understand, where did Mommy go? I don't understand what it means that she died." Barnhouse was trying to figure out how to explain death to his kids when, just then, a truck passed by and cast a shadow over the car. Barnhouse looked back at his kids and said, "Kids, would you rather have been hit by the truck or the shadow?" Well, of course, they would have rather been hit by the shadow, because the shadow doesn't hurt. Barnhouse then said, "Kids, when you die without Christ, you are hit by the truck. But, when you die with Christ, you are only hit by the shadow. The shadow is all you get."[18] Death holds no sting for the believer because we have so much to anticipate.

When we realize that there is so much that awaits us on the other side, death loses its sting. To wrap up this chapter, let me close with the following. Dream your wildest dreams about what the resurrected body and heaven will be like. Then, realize that your wildest dreams will not come close to the actualized glorious, reality that lies ahead. This makes me crave the return of Christ even more.

18. Evans, *Tony Evans' Book of Illustrations*, 72.

## Chapter Four

# WHAT DOES GOD LOOK LIKE?

*Rev. 1:9–18; 4:1–6a*

1. The Scene of the Source: God the Father (4:1–6a)

    a. *The Source's Power: Fiery presence*

    b. *The Source's Infinity: Emerald Light*

    c. *The Source's Faithfulness: Rainbow Encircling Throne*

    d. *The Source's Authority: Flashes of Lightning*

    e. *The Source's Personality: Seven Spirits-Holy Spirit*

    f. *The Source's Holiness: Sea of Glass*

2. The Scene of the Son (1:9–18)

    a. *Son's Unity: 7 Golden Lampstands*

    b. *Son's Authority: 4 Characteristics*

    c. *Son's Purity: White Hair and Clothing.*

    d. *Son's Supremacy: Awesome Strength, Bronzed Feet*

S ANDY'S TONE HAD BECOME far more relaxed when she realized all the amazing things that she would be able to do with the newly resurrected body. A tinge of giddiness could be detected as she reflected on the activities that she enjoyed doing that she hoped to be able to resume in the new body. Then, Sandy asked a big question. When I say a big question, I mean one of epic proportions. She said, "Brian, I have seen pictures of God being this old white man with a long white beard. Some people talk about God being a man, but others talk about God being a woman. When I think of the two sexes, I think about many of the compassionate women I have known who are sometimes more loving than men. What does God look like when we get there?"

As I prayerfully considered how to answer, I remembered a story that another lady from church told me—a lady named Pam Fulk. Pam was a loving woman who always sported an infectious smile. She told a story that involved a little girl in a Sunday school class. The teacher asked the students to draw a picture from the Bible. The teacher looked at one little girl's drawing. She asked, "What are you drawing?" The little girl said, "I'm drawing God." The teacher said, "Oh, honey. No one knows what God looks like." The little girl retorted, "Well, they will when I'm done." Quite a bold proclamation, indeed!

To answer Sandy's question, I first noted the idea of gender was futile when speaking of God, as God is spirit (John 4:24). The biblical language uses the term "Father," so that is the reason believers have traditionally used the masculine pronoun to reference God. Jesus was most certainly masculine. Thus, it only stands to reason that he would receive the masculine pronoun. Furthermore, Jesus called God his *Abba* (Matt. 6:9–13; Lk. 11:2–4), an Aramaic term meaning "Father." For that reason alone, God should retain the title "Father." However, I did not want to leave Sandy with a pat answer. To truly answer her question, my mind went back to John's vision of Jesus in Revelation 1:9–18.

The Spirit escorted John into heaven. John was guided to explain the things he witnessed. Throughout Revelation, John caught glimpses of heaven. However, the aged apostle focused on the vision he had of God in the first chapter. He detailed the appearance of Jesus in Revelation 1:9–18 and the appearance of God the Father in Revelation 5:1–6a. The citizenship is explained in Revelation 4:6b–11 and 7:9–10 and the New Jerusalem in Revelation 21 and 22. The citizenship of heaven and the New Jerusalem will serve as the focus of chapter 5. First, let us consider the view of God the Father from John's heavenly encounter.[1]

1. As was noted earlier, people cannot see God in their physical form and survive. However, John was permitted to have this vision of God. Did John have an out-of-body experience or was it merely a vision? One can only speculate. Regardless, God permitted John to see the things that he witnessed and was guided to record it in the book of

## The Scene of the Source: God the Father (4:1–6a)

Sandy was not the only one to inquire about how God appeared. A little girl at church asked the same question. I found it somewhat ironic that both Sandy and the little girl asked the same question within a matter of weeks. God is a spirit. Thus, God most likely does not appear as the long, gray-haired, bearded, muscle man in Michelangelo's creation portrait in the Sistine Chapel.

Thomas Aquinas contends that the best we can do when considering God's appearance or attributes is to use analogies to help us envision what God must be like.[2] While Aquinas's perspective is largely true, some aspects of God must be known univocally such as God's existence. Nonetheless, Aquinas was largely accurate in his assessment. This is perhaps the reason why Jesus and the biblical writers use analogies when depicting God. John was given an awe-inspiring vision of God the Father, one that puts all adventure movies to shame.

John is escorted to the very throne room of God while in the Spirit (4:2). He is overcome with awe. As you read these depictions, you will probably recall someone in your past who claimed that they plan to give God a piece of their mind when they see God face-to-face. Perhaps that person describes you. Yet when reading Revelation 4, it becomes fairly evident that the self-professed "big shots" of the world will not have as much to say as they think they will when they stand before the God of creation.

John sees God the Father seated on the throne, but he cannot quite make out the figure. He does observe some interesting aspects of God's presence. The text offers six characteristics about God in the text which denote God's power, infinity, faithfulness, authority, personality, and holiness.

### The Source's Power: Fiery Presence

First, the one seated on the throne had the appearance of "jasper and carnelian stone" (4:3a). The writer provides two gemstones to describe the divine presence. These gemstones would have stood out against the anthropomorphic demonstrations of the Greco-Roman pantheon of gods and goddesses.[3] It must be noted that the names of the gemstones sometimes differ from

Revelation for the believer's edification.

2. Aquinas, *Summa Theologica* I.q13.a.6.

3. Boxall, *Revelation of Saint John*, 84.

their modern titles. Often, this leaves the reader without a clear reference to the stone in question.[4] While we may not know the stones' identity with exact precision, we have good reasons for guessing what the writers inferred.

The first stone referenced is *jasper*. The jasper of today is an opaque gemstone that is usually mixed with iron giving it a red hue. However, it is more likely that John had in mind another stone. Commentators normally agree that John probably referred to a diamond illustrating the great intensity of God's light.[5] Jasper is listed first in the lists of gemstones (21:11, 18) and is at the head of the list of stones in the city walls of the New Jerusalem (21:19). The Johannine jasper links to the divine glory. Notice that in 21:11, the Johannine jasper shines like a crystal. Thus, this seems to suggest a diamond-like stone. However, the diamond may have had a bluish hue. Ancient rabbinic sages linked the color blue to the divine glory.[6] The Ark of the Covenant and items of the sanctuary were often covered with blue cloth when transported (Num. 4:6–12).[7] Some translations, such as the *Lexham English Bible,* interpret the presence of the angelic being in Daniel 10:6 with the color turquoise, which is normally labeled beryl as in the *Christian Standard Bible.* While blue diamonds were not discovered until the 17th century, it is not beyond the realm of possibility that John had in mind a diamond-like stone that gave off a bluish hue, much akin to the blue diamond. Certainly, this is speculation, but regardless of the hue, the crystalline stone would have shone like the brightness of the sun much like Ezekiel noted (Ezek. 1:28).

Additionally, God's presence is portrayed as a burning flame. God's fiery presence illustrates his intense, overwhelming power. Moses writes, "For the LORD your God is a consuming fire" (Deut. 4:24). The writer of Hebrews says the same, noting, "our God is a consuming fire" (Heb. 12:29). It is no surprise that God appeared to Moses in a burning bush (Ex. 3:2) and was a pillar of fire by night and a pillar of cloud by day, leading the Israelites away from captivity (Ex. 13:21–22). As Millard Erickson penned,

4. Easley, *Revelation,* 75.

5. Rydelnik and Vanlaningham, *Moody Bible Commentary,* 2007; "The former cannot be our 'jasper' which is opaque and colored and not a precious stone and thus does not fit 21:11, 'like to a stone most precious, as to a jasper stone of crystal clear splendor or brilliance,' which makes us think of nothing less than a diamond." Lenski, *Interpretation of St. John's Revelation,* 171.

6. *Numbers Rabbah* 14:3; *Hullin* 89a.

7. Frankel and Teutsch, *Encyclopedia of Jewish Symbols,* 22.

"Not only is omnipotence essential to worship, but only an almighty being can be a proper object of trust."[8]

One of my favorite past-times is sitting by the fire pit with a good flame ablaze. Especially when the flames are particularly hot, the interior of the flame holds a beautiful bluish complexion. Nuclear reactors also emit a beautiful, albeit eerie, bluish hue. Thus, it is feasible that the Johannine diamond of Revelation 4 could have also held such a color. What John saw would have been a dazzling scene of beauty and tremendous power. If John of Revelation is the same as the apostle, then the writer would have already posited that God is light (1 John 1:5). His dynamic vision would have verified his understanding of God's divine glory.

Contrasted with the crystalline bluish diamond, the *carnelian*, the second stone of John's vision of the divine glory, most likely was a deep, dark red; so dark that it almost looks black in some cases. The two gemstones illustrate the fiery presence of God. Consider the scene. The flashing diamond light with a bluish hue is juxtaposed with the blood-red carnelian stone. The majesty of God is enjoined with his holiness and judgment. As Lenski noted, "this is about as good as anyone can hope to envision with the text."[9]

One lady stated that this vision scared her as she was afraid of fire. I explained to her that the intensity of God's power must be held in connection with God's loving grace and mercy. God is still God. However, many, if not most, modern people have lost the sense of God's awesome power. Formerly, the phrase "a God-fearing person" was given as a compliment. The phrase identified the person as one who respected and revered God.

As one who has worked with electricity, I understand the importance of revering the power of electricity. This does not mean that a person does not work on electrical equipment because of their reverence, but that the person acknowledges the incredible and deadly power that electricity holds. A person's viewpoint of God should be the same. God's intense power is unlike anything ever conceived. The greatest natural power in the universe pales in comparison to God's unlimited power. Consider the power of cosmic nebulae and black holes. If a nebula (i.e., a stellar explosion) were to occur close enough to our planet, we would be instantly vaporized. Yet all the nebulae and black holes of the universe pale in comparison to God's awesome power. Rich Mullins was right, "Our God is an awesome God."

8. Erickson, *God the Father Almighty*, 165.

9. Lenski, *Interpretation of St. John's Revelation*, 171.

What do we take from this aspect of God's power? Remember, your problems are not too big for God. God is bigger than any difficulty that could be faced. We serve a God of possibilities. Do you have health problems? God raised the dead. Do you have financial problems? God owns everything and cares for his creation. Have you been mistreated? God judges all. No matter how big a problem is, God is always bigger.

## The Source's Infinity: Emerald Light

Second, John discovers an emerald-shaded rainbow encircling the throne of God (4:3). The divine presence depicted as gemstones illuminates out from the interior of God's Being. The rainbow holds significance, which we will discuss in a moment. But first, we must consider the color of the emerald and its significance.

Emeralds are dark green. Green is a color of life and eternity. Jeremiah compares the person who trusts in the LORD to a tree "planted by water: it sends its roots out towards the stream, it doesn't fear when the heat comes, and its foliage remains green. It will not worry in a year of drought or cease producing fruit" (Jer. 17:8). While John's primary image is of God's awesome light, the emerald's green hue is significant for two reasons.

First, it denotes God's eternal attributes. God has no beginning and no end. When approaching God, the person approaches One who is not constrained by space and time. God is both transcendent, existing outside of time, and immanent, existing in time.[10] Seeing that God is unrestrained by time, one can deduce that God's timetable is always right while acknowledging God's moral character.

Second, God never changes. Societies change. People change. Cultures change. Anyone who survived the crazy year of 2020 will note how quickly everything seemed to change from one day to the next. Regardless of the changes experienced in life, God consistently remains the same. He is the same yesterday, today, and forever (Heb. 13:8). His eternal and immutable nature should bring us hope.

10. Erickson sees this view as an acceptable view of God and time. Erickson, *God the Father Almighty*, 139.

## The Source's Faithfulness: Rainbow Encircling Throne

Third, one moves to the rainbow encircling the throne of God. The rainbow is a perfect circle surrounding God's throne. The emerald hue does not restrain the remaining colors of God's rainbow of light as it is only the hue outside the rainbow. It may seem strange at first notice to read about the circularity of God's rainbow. Rainbows often appear semicircular. Ironically, rainbows are only semicircular because land blocks the bottom half of the circle. When viewed from an aircraft, the complete circularity of the rainbow can be seen. Rainbows are produced when light is refracted and dispersed by rain or other droplets in the atmosphere. Interestingly, God's presence is often manifested in Scripture by light, clouds, fire, or a combination of the three.[11] The rainbow John sees could be the interaction of God's light with the cloud of his Shekinah glory.

Biblically, rainbows depict God's covenants with humanity. After the great flood, God made a promise to humanity to never again destroy the world by water (Gen. 9:1–17). The next global judgment would come by fire. God then sealed his covenant with Noah with a rainbow in the sky. While the vision of John depicts the glory of God as he is, the rainbow also serves as a reminder of God's faithfulness. Apocalyptic literature like the book of Revelation was never intended to be scary or frightening. The goal of the apocalyptic genre was to provide hope to those who were hurting. To encapsulate the symbolic nature of the rainbow, one should be reminded that God can be trusted in all the promises that he grants. As previously noted, God cannot lie (Titus 1:2) and cannot perform evil actions (1 John 1:5). Thus, God will neither lie nor manipulate. He is trustworthy in all that he says and does.

## The Source's Judgment: Flashes of Lightning

Fourth, lightning bolts flash from the presence of God. The energy and power of God are intense and unlike any storm you have ever witnessed. Lightning continuously flashes from God's awesome presence resulting in loud intense thunder (4:5). God's presence is sheer power and energy. Some authors posit that the occurrences of lightning should not be taken in any literal sense. For instance, the *Eerdman's Dictionary of the Bible* posits that "Lightning (Heb. *bārāq*; Gk. *astrapē*) is most often used in the Bible

---

11. See the article "Theophanies" in Barry, *Lexham Bible Dictionary*.

not in a literal sense but as an analogy to represent power, brilliance, and quickness."[12] While agreeing with the analogous aspects of lightning, a degree of literal interpretation is warranted. In Zechariah, Yahweh's arrows of judgment go forth like lightning (Zech. 9:14). Yahweh answered Elijah's prayer to strike down the enemy captains and their armies with fire from heaven, which was most likely lightning (2 Kgs. 1:10–12). Yahweh's presence on Mount Sinai was accompanied by thunder and flashes of lightning (Exod. 20:18). Lightning accompanies powerful forms of energy in biblical literature. If God is held to hold great power and energy, it is not beyond the realm of possibility that lightning could, and likely does, exude from his awesome might.

While possibly literal in its depiction of God, lightning and thunder symbolically remind the reader of God's awesome power and just nature. Some judges can be bribed to dismiss the guilty and permit them to re-enter society. However, God will never be bribed. God can never be manipulated. Seriously, how do you expect to bribe someone who owns everything? How do you expect to manipulate someone who knows all there is to know? It is impossible.

Divine lightning holds a special place in my heart because of the two ways in which God used lightning to steer me in the right direction. This is part of the reason why I am open to the idea of lightning exuding from God's glorious presence. The first occurrence happened on September 17, 1993. This was the date that my grandmother, Eva Chilton, passed away. I had previously read in a *Guideposts* magazine how a young man asked God for a sign to reassure him that a loved one who had passed was okay. He asked God to send a bolt of lightning indicating that the dearly departed resided in heaven. God answered the man's prayer. I thought to myself, "Well, if God did it for him, maybe he will do it for me." I was not expecting God to do anything. But I asked the Lord, "God, I realize it is almost the fall of the year. But if you could send a lightning bolt to indicate that my grandma is okay, I would greatly appreciate it."

That evening, the family was gathered at my grandparents' home. I was sitting at one corner of the house while my grandfather and Rev. Gilmer Denny, a beloved friend of the family, sat at the other corner. As I sat, looking out the window at the night sky, it happened. Bolts of lightning struck just outside both corners of the home filling the house with a dazzling electric blue hue. I initially did not consider the prayer previously

12. Freedman, *Eerdmans Dictionary of the Bible*, 810.

prayed. I was too stunned. Everyone in the house jumped and began to examine the house to ensure that nothing was damaged. Then, it occurred to me, as if someone had planted the thought in my head, I had prayed for God to send a sign by lightning. God delivered the sign in an impressive display of power. To this day, I do not know whether one lightning bolt split and struck outside the home, or whether two lightning bolts struck simultaneously. All that I do know is that God vividly answered my prayers. My grandmother was safe in the arms of Jesus.

Second, God used lightning to bring me back into the gospel ministry. Fast-forward fourteen years to July of 2007. God had radically delivered me from agnosticism back to Christian theism. Yet, God impressed upon my mind the need to re-enter Christian ministry. I fought it for quite some time. On one fateful day, God got my attention in a way that I never saw coming. I was in my outdoor building getting in a weightlifting workout. Without warning, a powerful and dangerous thunderstorm hit our area. Lightning popped around the building. Attempts to run back to the house were thwarted by dangerous bolts which shook the ground around me.

Surrounded by weightlifting plates, bars, and machines all made of metal, metal lawnmowing equipment, and water-absorbent poplar trees, I had unintentionally become a lightning rod inviting the dazzling streaks of fire to enter my body. The hairs on my body began to rise, a clear sign that a strike was imminent. The lightning was close enough that it could be smelled. Yes, lightning has a smell. It smells like burnt plastic wires. The only thing left for me to do was pray. "God, help me! Get me out of this situation!" I pleaded. The storm did not immediately cease after I prayed, yet a peace came upon me as if to tell me that everything was going to be fine. I remained in the kneeling position as I continued to pray.

The storm left as quickly as it came. Stepping outside of the building, I had a new perspective, especially when I looked behind the building. A lightning bolt had struck just outside the building where I was located, leaving behind a large gaping hole about five inches in diameter. God may not always remove us from the storms, but he will protect us within the storms.

With the amazing display of God's protective power, it was a cinch for me to accept God's calling back into the ministry. I shared this story with Sandy. She also acknowledged how God had helped her through many storms in her life. What storm can stand against a God whose dazzling glory produces flashes of intense lightning? What storm can oppose a God who owns the copyright to all that exists? Additionally, if lightning from an earthly storm could put this Southern boy on his face, one can only imagine the illuminating, overpowering, radiant, emblazing, intense, dazzling, electrifying presence of the Almighty Creator of the cosmos. Storms may terrify us. But storms are terrified by the presence of God. If God is for you, what storm can be against you? Can you envision what the awesome glory of God will be like? As the popular song asserts, I can only imagine.

## The Source's Personality: Seven Spirits

Fifth, John views "seven fiery torches . . . burning before the throne, which are the seven spirits of God" (4:5). Again, there may be an element of literal interpretation as John would have seen something like flames of fire burning around the throne of God. He identifies the flames with a personality. The flames do not represent an impersonal entity but rather a personal deity. While symbols may contain some literal element to their depictions, symbolic interpretation assists the expositor to identify what, or rather whom, the text references. The interpreter needs to examine three symbolic identifiers at this junction: flames, seven, and spirits.

First, consider the depiction of flames. Fire is often associated with divine manifestations, called *theophanies*.[13] God appeared as a flaming torch when he established a covenant with Abraham (Gen. 15:17), as a flame of fire within a burning bush when encountering Moses (Exod. 3:2), as a pillar of fire by night when leading the Hebrews toward the Promised Land (Exod. 13:21–22), and as fire on Mount Sinai when giving the law to Moses (Exod. 19:18). In the NT, the Holy Spirit descends as "tongues of fire" on the early church (Acts 2:3). Additionally, Christ appears with blazing attire and possessing eyes as flames of fire (Rev. 1:14; 2:18). Fire describes God's holy action and his protective nature when linked to God's works (Zech. 2:5). God purifies by fire which sometimes includes national purging (Ps. 66:12; Isa. 43:2). The Day of the Lord will be a time when God purifies Israel (Zech. 13:9; 1 Cor. 3:13–15). Thus, fire denotes the holy and righteous nature of God. God himself is a "consuming fire" (Heb. 12:29; Deut. 4:24).

Second, the number seven is important to consider. The number seven represented completeness and perfection.[14] God created the universe in seven days (Gen. 1:1—2:4). Individuals were to have a sabbath each week and the land was to have a sabbath each seventh year (Lev. 25:2–7). Pharaoh

13. Achtemeier, *Harper's Bible Dictionary*, 309.
14. Achtemeier, *Harper's Bible Dictionary*, 711.

saw seven good years and seven years of famine in his vision (Gen. 41:1–36). Jacob worked seven years for Rachel and seven more years when Laban fooled him by giving Leah instead (Gen. 29:15–30). Psalm 12:6 argues that the finest quality silver was refined seven times. In the NT, the number seven is seen in the number of churches exhorted in Revelation 2–3 and the number of deacons first chosen (Acts 6:1–6). Additionally, Jesus said that a person was to forgive 70 times 7 times a day (Matt. 18:21–22). Multiples of seven were introduced in the biblical text. The year of Jubilee was a time when all debts were forgiven, and all bondservants were released. This came after the completion of 49 years (7x7) (Lev. 25:8–55). God instructed Moses to choose 70 elders (Exod. 24:1, 9), and Jesus sent out 70 disciples two by two to preach in his name (Luke 10:1–17). The nation of Israel was in exile for 70 years (Jer. 25:12; 29:10; Dan. 9:2). Daniel prophesied a timetable of messianic events using 70 weeks (Dan. 9:24). Thus, the use of seven denotes the complete and perfect nature of the entity in question.

Finally, note the presence of spirits. Since we have already defined the terms *ruach* and *pneuma* used for "spirit," it is unnecessary to repeat that exercise here.[15] The term "spirit" is held to describe a personal and living entity. Hence, the seven spirits of fire do not describe an inanimate object, but rather describe a personal, living being.

Combining the aspect of fire, the number seven, and the personal aspect of the spirit; one can safely assess that the "seven spirits of God" which are the "seven spirits of God" (Rev. 4:5) denote the living presence of the Holy Spirit. Jesus ascribes the role of Counselor to the Holy Spirit (John 14:16). The Spirit of God intercedes for believers and even prays for the child of God when the individual does not know what to pray for oneself (Rom. 8:26). This same Spirit is found at the throne of God. Unsurprising really when considering that the Spirit is God.

The Holy Spirit represents not only the Third Person of the Trinity but also that God is personal in his nature. While he is awesome in his presence and holds inexplicable power, this God is also loving, kind, and approachable in establishing relationships. If you think you do not have a friend, think again. The awesome, majestic Creator of the universe has offered a relationship to you, through his Son, Jesus Christ.

---

15. See the discussion on the spiritual body and the definition of *pneuma* and *ruach* given there.

## The Source's Holiness: Sea of Glass

Sixth and finally, below the throne of God is found a "sea of glass, similar to crystal, . . . before the throne" (4:6a). The big question is, what is this sea of glass? The sea of glass represents two things: 1) God's holiness, and 2) God's victory over evil. The sea is a symbol of chaos and evil which will be discussed a bit later. The calmness of the sea of glass indicates that God's holy nature has completely vanquished evil. Evil cannot abide in the same presence of God. Some may think, "Ah, evil must somehow corrupt God in some fashion." That is not the case. God's holiness is so powerful that he must either purify evil or destroy it whenever something evil approaches him. The presence of God vaporizes evil when the two come in contact. The OT and NT both heavily emphasize the absolute holiness of God. This means that God is the absolute good, he can do no evil. God is the absolute truth; he tells no lies. God is the absolute light; he has no darkness whatsoever. God is the absolute power; he has no weakness.

In like manner, this sea, deep blue like the lapis lazuli stone, represents God's complete defeat of evil. In an oft-forgotten biblical text, God met with Moses, Aaron, Nadab, Abihu, and the 70 elders of Israel by a theophanic manifestation. Wherever God walked, the ground turned to lapis lazuli (Exod. 24:10)—a deep, dark blue.

As I described the blue sea of glass beneath the throne of God, Sandy asked a question that had often plagued my mind. She stated, "The Bible says that in heaven there will be no more sea. I have always loved going to the ocean. Does that mean that heaven will not have any bodies of water?" She referenced Revelation 21:1 which states that "the first heaven and the first earth had passed away, and the sea was no more." At this juncture, it is important to understand how the Bible metaphorically describes the sea. Ancients viewed the sea as a place of chaos. Storms and underwater beasts often threatened seafarers as they sailed across the seas. Thus, the sea was vastly unstable compared to the steadfast security of the ground. God brings peace and calm from the chaos of the storm.[16] Because the people failed to repent, Isaiah professes that God would bring the chaos of the mighty rushing waters of judgment against them (Isa. 8:6). In contrast, God establishes peace and serenity from the chaos for those who trust in him (Isa. 33:21–24).

---

16. Rydelnik and Vanlaningham, *Moody Bible Commentary,* 2026.

The absence of the sea is metaphorical. It points back to the security that Yahweh brought to his covenant people. Likewise, heaven is a place without chaos. God establishes perfect peace and serenity in his new creation. Human depravity and the enemies of darkness bring about chaos and uncertainty. The citizens of heaven will be purified from sin; thus, sin will hold no impact. Furthermore, the enemies of darkness will have been subdued and locked away from this new creation leaving them with no impact in this place. From the heavenly depiction of an Edenic garden, water is shown to flow from the throne of God. Thus, water will exist in heaven. If the physical seas are a source of beauty now, the bodies of water in heaven will be even more splendid.

I do not think that John addresses physical seas and oceans in Revelation 21. I think he points to the metaphorical contrast between peace and chaos. Chaos will not exist in heaven. Consider God's absolute goodness, perfection, and purity. Now realize, your thoughts about God's goodness, perfection, and purity do not even come close to the reality of those divine attributes. Now that God's awesome presence has been considered, one's attention is now turned to the appearance of the Son.

## The Scene of the Son (1:9–18)

Have you ever noticed that when Jesus is celebrated it is normally in a weakened state? At Christmas, people celebrate Jesus as a babe lying in a manger. He is weak and powerless in this state. On Good Friday, believers contemplate the sacrifice that Jesus made on the cross. But even then, Jesus is in a state of weakness having been tortured and left for dead. Even the crosses Christians erect depict him in a weakened state.

Yet the vision of Jesus in heaven is a far cry from the weakened Jesus depicted in popular art. John not only describes the characteristics of the Father, but he also describes the characteristics of the Son as he encounters Jesus up-close and personal in Jesus's new heavenly state. No longer is he a harmless baby. No longer is he a victim on a cross. Now he exudes power and strength. The vision in the book of Revelation reveals four amazing characteristics found in this heavenly Jesus—the Jesus found in heaven.

## Son's Unity: Golden Lampstands

First, John describes Jesus standing among seven golden lampstands. He writes, "Then I turned to see whose voice it was that spoke to me. When I turned I saw seven golden lampstands, and among the lampstands was one like the Son of Man, dressed in a robe and with a golden sash wrapped around his chest" (Rev. 1:12–13). Jesus appears among seven golden lampstands. The number seven, as previously noted, represents completion or perfection. It could also represent the totality of a referenced thing. That is to say, the seven golden lampstands represent not just a number but the total of the lampstands' reference. Thus, one must inquire, what do the lampstands symbolize?

Thankfully, the solution to the lampstand conundrum is given in Revelation 1:20. Jesus says, "The mystery of the seven stars you saw in my right hand and of the seven golden lampstands is this: The seven stars are the angels of the seven churches, and the seven lampstands are the seven churches" (Rev. 1:20). The lampstands are the seven churches. But why did Jesus select only seven churches to address in Revelation 2–3? Certainly, many more churches existed than just the seven churches of Asia Minor. Reading the epistles of Paul, additional early churches were identified, such as the Church of Corinth, Galatia, Rome, and Thessalonica. Perhaps these were churches under John's watch care? Perhaps these churches represent seven types of churches? Some commentators contend that the epistles to the seven churches are a "literary microcosm of the entire book's macrocosmic structure."[17] The seven churches could represent seven historical phases of the church leading to the return of Christ. Whatever the case may be, it does appear that the seven churches represent something larger than themselves, perhaps even the totality of the church as a whole.

The most important image is Jesus standing among the seven lampstands. Even now, Jesus is united with the churches, united as we stand, and helps us as we fall. The image of Jesus with the lampstands recalls another powerful image in the book of Zechariah. The prophet Zechariah (c. 520 BC) is guided through a visionary experience himself. He sees a divine being, perhaps Jesus or an angelic figure, who serves as a guide through his visionary experience. The visionary guide asks Zechariah to identify what he sees. Zechariah replies, "I see a solid golden lampstand with a bowl at the top. The lampstand also has seven lamps at the top with seven spouts for

---

17. Beale, *Book of Revelation*, 224.

each of the lamps. There are also two olive trees beside it, one on the right of the bowl and the other on its left" (Zech. 4:2–3). The oil is identified as the anointed ones later in the chapter (Zech. 4:14). The symbol requires a lot of unpacking, much of which would detract from the focus of our current goal. However, it should be noted that the lampstands have a continuous stream of oil provided by the olive trees feeding them. The overall context suggests that the lampstands represent the people of God.

Some may read Zechariah's vision and think that it is too far-fetched for the purposes intended by Jesus and the church in Revelation 1. However, recall that Jesus taught, "I am the vine; you are the branches. The one who remains in me and I in him produces much fruit, because you can do nothing without me" (John 15:5). Jesus is connected to his church. Likewise, the church is interconnected.

Western individualism may struggle to conceive the interconnectedness that believers have with Christ and with one another. However, the interconnectedness of believers is something espoused in the pages of Scripture. Jesus does not say that he only fuels one believer. He fuels us all. Paul taught that believers have various gifts to help one another and ultimately benefit Christ's church (1 Cor. 12:21).

The vision of Jesus among the lampstands should remind us of two things. First, the Triune God only deserves to be worshiped. The Father initiated our salvation, the Son enacted it, and the Spirit connects us. Second, remember that we are united as a church for all eternity. When one member succeeds, we all rise together. When one fails, we all hurt. However, when people fall, we do not stand to crucify the person. By doing so, we crucify ourselves. Rather, we should try to uplift the person. Like the interconnected roots of a forest, so the church is united in the blessed union of Christ. In heaven, our Shepherd, King, and Friend walks among us and fellowships with us. The church is the bride of Christ (Rev. 21:2, 9; 2 Cor. 11:2). The church will be united with Christ forever.

## Son's Authority: Four Characteristics

Second, Jesus exhibits traits that denote his power and authority in heaven. Four characteristics point to Jesus's divine authority in eternity. First, he dons a "golden sash wrapped around his chest" (Rev. 1:13) as he stands among the lampstands. Gold is a color of royalty and divinity. The sash represents the authority of his position. Jesus's attire points to his position as both a king and a priest. He serves as a ruler in eternity and serves as the high priest. The messianic priest-king role was prophesied in Zechariah and fulfilled in Christ.

Second, Jesus is shown to have "eyes like a fiery flame" (Rev. 1:14). Fire is a symbol of the energy and presence of Almighty God. Fire also represents judgment. The eyes are the instrument by which the world is viewed. Putting the two concepts together, the fiery eyes represent Christ's ability to see things the way they are. He is not fooled and is not mistaken. He not only sees the exterior of a person's being but also peers into the very soul. Not even one's thoughts are off limits. Christ knows all and sees all.

Let us give an additional comment about the eyes of Christ before we move to the next symbol. Throughout history, people have placed a high value on appearances. Educators encourage students to look their best when attending school so that they will be prepared to look their best when interviewing for jobs. The fashion industry is a multi-million, if not multi-billion, dollar conglomerate enterprise that focuses on exterior beauty. The emphasis we place on external appearances often leads people to wear masks in their conduct. By these masks, we do not mean literal masks such as one may find at Halloween or Mardi Gras. Rather, the masks we refer to here are the psychological masks that are worn.

For instance, a person may behave a certain way in certain locations and behave completely differently when at home. I recall a coworker who was the most talkative person when on the floor. But at a Christmas party that his wife also attended, he hardly uttered a word—to the shock of everyone present. Our coworker behaved one way at work and another at home. When Christ looks at us, he is not impressed with our external appearance. He is not impressed by our physical strength or mental prowess. Why would he when he is omnipotent and omniscient? When Christ looks at us, he does not see only the external person, but rather he peers into the soul of humanity. Christ sees us as we truly are. No mask can filter his sight.

The third and fourth symbols both relate to the power of Christ's spoken word. In verse 15, his voice is likened to "cascading waters" indicating the authority of his words. The late Adrian Rogers had a tremendous speaking voice. His baritone voice thundered across the microphone with great crispness and clarity. I often sound like a bumbling fool when I try to speak because I have so many thoughts coming to mind and not enough tongue to get them out. Although my wife has often accused me of having a big mouth, sometimes it is difficult to get my words out. As powerful as

Rogers's voice may have been, the voice of God thunders with the greatest impact when he speaks. No speaker could ever match the awesome vocal communicative ability of the Sovereign God. The best human speakers are only but a foretaste of the amazing voice of God.

Finally, in verse 15, Jesus is shown to have a "double-edged sword" coming from his mouth, representing the authority Jesus holds to cast judgment and execute judgment. Jesus possesses ultimate authority. He can see things the way they are, not buying into flimsy excuses and illogical arguments. He is not like judges who let criminals go Scott-free. Christ judges righteously and his verdict is final.

Revelation 1:14 connects with the prophecy of Psalm 110:1 which speaks of the Messiah being near to Almighty God. The imagery is also found in Daniel 7:13–14 where the one like a Son of Man (Aram., *bar enash*) approaches the Ancient of Days. The imagery of Revelation 1:14 describes Jesus holding ultimate authority over all things. Jesus has the authority not only to speak, but to enact his judgments because his authority is complete, his decisions are just, and his judgments are final. J. I. Packer wisely notes, "Christians take great comfort in knowing that Christ is Lord of all; they seek in every sphere of life to do his will and to remind themselves and others that all are accountable to Christ as Judge, whether they be governors or governed, husbands or wives, parents or children, employers or employees."[18] Every sphere of life is governed and under the subjection of Christ's authority. If this is understood, the way the world and life are viewed is radically transformed.

Too often, believers are overly inundated with the concerns of the world. Jesus even noted that his kingdom is not of this world (John 18:36). While his kingdom is not of this world, his kingdom overrules this world. There is no doubt that Jesus is loving and kind. However, we also must remember that he is the King of kings and Lord of lords. Millard Erickson asserts that Christ "is not merely the highest of the creatures, but is God in the same sense and to the same degree as the Father. He is as deserving of our praise, adoration, and obedience as is the Father."[19] Erickson concludes, "One day everyone will recognize who and what Jesus is."[20] We must all ask ourselves; do we place more trust in human authorities than we do in the ultimate authority of God? One way to gauge this level of trust is to see how

18. Packer, *Concise Theology*, 130.
19. Erickson, *Christian Theology*, 642.
20. Erickson, *Christian Theology*, 642.

much time is spent talking about Christ as opposed to political issues and political leaders.

## Son's Purity: White Hair and Clothing

John continues his description by attributing Jesus with hair "white as wool—white as snow" (1:14). The color white indicates purity and great wisdom. Jesus is perfect. He is of absolute purity and holiness. He can and will do no wrong. When a person is deemed trustworthy, you can trust what that person says, in contrast to a person who lies all the time. What Jesus has promised, he will fulfill. When Jesus's divine nature is accepted, then one acknowledges that Jesus cannot lie since the same applies to God. This has been previously noted but deserves to be re-emphasized, it is not just that God chooses not to lie, it is an impossibility for God to lie (Titus 1:2).

Too often, believers idolize human leaders as miniature saviors. The adulation given to leaders often borders on the idolatrous. When these leaders fail or fall, the believer suffers great despair. As portions of this book were being written, a conservative presidential candidate failed to receive enough votes to retain his Presidency. The level of sorrow witnessed among believers who prophetically claimed that this person would retain his Presidency was astounding. It leads one to ask whether the worship deserved by Jesus alone was not also given to political candidates, and this is true for candidates on both sides of the political aisle.

We wonder why such turmoil has overtaken our world. But when our political and religious leaders are given such adoration, they rob the worship that so deservedly belongs to Christ. These leaders cannot offer the character and integrity that Jesus affords. Furthermore, there is a biblical word that describes the practice of someone and/or something receiving the worship that belongs to God—*idolatry.*

Another form of idolatry is found with the glorification of Christian leaders, RZIM issued a statement noting the ongoing investigation led them to accept that the charges of Ravi Zacharias's moral indiscretions proved to be true.[21] Providing that the reports were true, Zacharias's moral fall impacted me most because he was a hero of mine. I benefited greatly from his writings, lectures, and teachings. However, Ravi was still a human being. He was not the Savior. The people who knew Jesus best compared him to an "unblemished and spotless lamb" (1 Pet. 1:18). Even Paul who was formerly

21. Update from RZIM Board: Allegations Against Ravi Zacharias | RZIM.

an enemy of Jesus wrote, "For our sake he made him to be sin who knew no sin, so that in him we might become the righteousness of God" (2 Cor. 5:21, ESV). Ravi's moral failings remind us that the true object of our worship must be the Triune God alone. No one else is worthy of that worship.

Christ had to be perfect to save us from our sins. If Jesus was a sinner, then his death was only atoned for his own sins. He had to be perfect to bear our sins upon his back. As Wayne Grudem notes, "For this reason, Christ had to live a life of perfect obedience to God in order to earn righteousness for us. He had to obey the law for his whole life on our behalf so that the positive merits of his perfect obedience would be counted for us."[22] If for no other reason, Christians should worship only the Triune God because of what he has done for us. The Father was the Source, the Sender, and the Planner of salvation;[23] the Son was the Means, Sent One, and Achiever of salvation;[24] and the Holy Spirit is the Effector, the Proceeded One, and Applier of salvation to each individual.[25] Salvation truly involved each Person of the Triune Godhead. No politician or worship leader could ever do for you what God has already done. If you believe that, then why do you place such emphasis on the things of the world? As the aged apostle John asserts, "Do not love the world or the things in the world. If anyone loves the world, the love of the Father is not in him" (1 John 2:15).[26] No politician can escort you across the threshold of death and into eternity. Only God, and God alone, can.

## Son's Supremacy: Awesome Strength, Bronzed Feet

In his new resurrected state, Jesus is shown to hold incredible strength. John shows Jesus's feet likened to "fine bronze as it is fired in a furnace" (1:15). Bronze was an alloy of copper and tin, and stronger than both. Bronze was used for armor (1 Sam. 17:5–6), shackles (2 Kgs. 25:7), cymbals (1 Chr. 15:19), and gates (Ps. 107:16). Bronze was known for its incredible strength which gave any military that could produce bronzed items a decisive advantage over other armies that did not have access to bronze plating. When John compares Jesus's feet to bronze, it could be that he was

22. Grudem, *Systematic Theology,* 707.

23. Geisler, *Systematic Theology: In One Volume,* 549.

24. Geisler, *Systematic Theology: In One Volume,* 549.

25. Geisler, *Systematic Theology: In One Volume,* 549.

26. John reiterated the message that Jesus had previously given (Matt. 6:24).

describing Jesus's Middle Eastern olive-toned skin. But, more likely, John is describing Jesus's supreme and awesome strength.

As a lifelong fan of Marvel comics, one of my favorite characters has always been the Incredible Hulk. I particularly love the way the comic books and television shows, featuring Lou Ferrigno and Bill Bixby, portray the Hulk over the cinematic adaptations. Banner often tried to help individuals in need. However, he found himself and others being abused by bullies and power-hungry narcissists. When he became angry, he turned into the raging Hulk who was able to right wrongs and bring justice to the oppressed. The only problem with the Hulk is that his emotions often led him to do things that he never desired.

In contrast with the Hulk, the actual Jesus of heaven has limitless power. He will right the wrongs of the oppressed. He stands for the rights of the weak and stands opposed to the bullies of the world—the ultimate bully being the devil. In his heavenly state, Jesus holds power that far exceeds any fictional comic book hero. Jesus, as he exists in his new heavenly state, is not the pasty-skinned, anemic, hippy that is often portrayed in the most well-intentioned movies. Rather, Jesus is the conqueror, defender, and redeemer. He is the cornerstone by which the redeemed find their strength, and from which tyrants are crushed.

## Conclusion

This chapter has examined the attributes of God and how he will most likely appear in heaven. Even with the attempted descriptions afforded in this section, we must realize that even the biblical depictions of God pale in comparison to how God will actually appear. The reason why the biblical writers had to use allegories and symbols is due to the incomparable attributes of God.

The largest planet in our solar system, Jupiter, is viewable on most evenings. It is one of the brightest objects in the night sky. When viewed through a telescope, one observes a red spot on the planet which is known as the Great Red Spot. Rather than being just a spot, the red image on the planet is a massive hurricane! Scientists believe that the outer bands of the storm produce winds of around 268 miles-per-hour, over 100 miles-an-hour greater than some of the strongest recorded hurricanes on earth![27]

---

27. Rogers, *Giant Planet Jupiter*, 195.

Even the power of the greatest planetary and cosmological entities cannot come close to the power of God.

For some, images of divine fire, lightning, and power can evoke fear. This was the case with Sandy. Instead of providing comfort, she was intimidated by awe-inspiring images of an awesome Being with limitless power. I steered her back to the moral attributes of God. I reminded her that as an Anselmian Being—that which nothing greater could be conceived—God is the absolute good, which indicates that God desires the absolute best for us all. As such, his power ensures that his goodness can reach beyond any obstacle that the Enemy may place in his way.

Concerning Jesus, he is often remembered for his stages of weakness. Jesus, as he now stands, holds absolute power and strength. He is not beaten nor is he the babe in a manger. He is a conqueror who has been victorious over death, hell, the grave, and your sin. With all this in mind, we can conclude along with Dr. Steven Gaines, former SBC president, who stated, "I'm a nobody, who loves Somebody, Who died for everybody, and Who can save anybody."[28]

---

28. Obtained from a message by Dr. Stephen Gaines on his social media account.

## Chapter Five

# WHAT WILL HEAVEN LOOK LIKE?

*Rev. 1:9–18; 4:1–11; 7:9–10; 21:9–14, 22–27; 22:1–5;*
*Rev. 1:9–18; 4:1–6a; Isa. 11:1–9*

1. The Scene of the Citizens (4:6b–11; 7:9–10)

   a. *The Angelic Citizens (4:6b–11)*

   b. *The Human Citizens (7:9–10)*

   c. *The Animal Citizens (Isa. 11:1–9)*

2. The Scene of the City (21:9–14, 22–27; 22:1–5)

   a. *The City's Connection (21:9–23)*

   b. *The City's Holiness (21:24–27)*

   c. *The City's Life (22:1–3a)*

S ANDY'S FEARS CONCERNING GOD'S awesome appearance were alleviated when we discussed God's goodness. However, her concerns quickly faded when thinking about what heaven would be like. She wanted to know how heaven would appear, but she also had another perplexing problem that lingered in her mind, a problem that many have often considered. That topic concerns who and/or what will be found in heaven. Before we get to Sandy's most-pressing question, let's consider the sights and sounds of this new heavenly abode. To catch a glimpse of the wonders awaiting us in heaven, it proves necessary to look at John's depiction of heaven in Revelation as well as the images found in Isaiah chapter 11. As we look through the material, keep in mind that just as God is that Being by which nothing greater can be conceived, so also will God's heaven be that place by which nothing greater can be conceived. Before looking at the conditions of the heavenly abode, let us first consider the heavenly citizens—that is, those beings found in God's new creation.

## The Scene of the Citizens (4:6b–11; 7:9–10)

Who are the citizens found in heaven? By citizens, we speak of the beings and creatures found in this new heavenly creation. Are there only a specific number of individuals who will enter heaven, or will there be an enormous number of heavenly citizens? We discover two kinds of heavenly citizens: angelic citizens and human citizens. Additionally, one finds that heaven is a place brimming with life as we will soon discover.

### The Angelic Citizens (4:6b–11)

In the last chapter, we were introduced to the throne room of God. We witnessed the great power and grandeur of God. In this chapter, we want to look at the beings surrounding God's throne and the occupants of this new heavenly abode. Revelation 4:6–11 tells us the following:

> 6 Something like a sea of glass, similar to crystal, was also before the throne. Four living creatures covered with eyes in front and in back were around the throne on each side. 7 The first living creature was like a lion; the second living creature was like an ox; the third living creature had a face like a man; and the fourth living creature was like a flying eagle. 8 Each of the four living creatures had six wings; they were covered with eyes around and inside. Day and night they never stop, saying,
>
> Holy, holy, holy,
> Lord God, the Almighty,
> who was, who is, and who is to come.
>
> 9 Whenever the living creatures give glory, honor, and thanks to the one seated on the throne, the one who lives forever and ever, 10 the twenty-four elders fall down before the one seated on the throne and worship the one who lives forever and ever. They cast their crowns before the throne and say,

[11] Our Lord and God,
you are worthy to receive
glory and honor and power,
because you have created all things,
and by your will
they exist and were created (Rev. 4:6–11).

Surrounding God's throne, one finds the mighty, yet somewhat bi-zarre-looking creatures known as the cherubim. They are but one of the numerous varieties of angelic beings. These massive beings have the face of a lion, an ox, a human, and an eagle. Each has six wings, able to see every point around them. The eyes are symbolic of the beings' ability to see all around them. They are creatures of great wisdom. But they are not the only beings found in heaven. The Bible indicates that there will be several forms of angelic entities. Of particular interest are the cherubim, seraphim, arch-angels, guardian angels, and the angelic order mentioned in the Pauline epistles. Let's take a closer look at them.

*Seraphim:* Isaiah describes the seraph as a fiery creature that could have a human form with serpentine qualities. It appears that the seraphim are agents of purification and, like the cherubim, are worship leaders. One ancient depiction of the angel is found in a sculpture found at Tell Halaf dated 800 BC, which depicts the seraph as having a human body, two wings at the shoulders and four below the waist. In Isaiah, a seraph takes a lump of hot coal to purify Isaiah's lips so that he can approach God's throne (Isa. 6:1–7). Since seraphim are serpentine creatures, it has been held by some that Satan could be a fallen seraph, although some have held that Satan is more likely a fallen cherub.[1]

*Cherubim:* Cherubim are attendants to God's throne. Cherubim also guarded the tree of life. Thus, the cherub serves as a sentinel in many re-spects. These creatures are massive and quite odd in appearance. It appears that they can see in all directions and, according to Ezekiel, roll on some type of wheeled apparatus that allows them to move as fast as lightning. It seems that the cherubim not only guard God's holiest places, but they also conduct the throne room in worship. Ironically, the cherubim stand mark-edly different from the popular images ascribed to them. Cherubim are

---

1. Michael Heiser contends that Satan was a fallen cherub. Heiser, *Unseen Realm*, 81–82, 243, 281. However, it is difficult to discount the parallels between the seraphim and the serpentine imagery of the Satan figure in Scripture. In either case, Satan was an angel of extreme prominence before his fall.

often shown to be cute, cuddly, babies with wings. Scripture depicts these creatures far removed from their popular imagery.

*Archangels:* The Bible lists two archangels: Gabriel and Michael. Gabriel is the herald of God, while Michael is a warrior angel who defends the people of God. Extra-biblical literature, even found in the Apocrypha, notes that there are seven archangels. The highest four archangels are Gabriel (Dan. 8:16; 1 En. 9:1; 20:7; 40:9), Michael (Jude 9; Dan. 10:13; 12:1; 1 En. 9:1; 10:11), Raphael (Tob. 3:17; 12:14; 1 En. 10:4; 40:9), and Uriel (1 En. 9:1; 19:1; 20:2). *1 Enoch* lists the remaining three archangels as Saraquel, Raguel, and Remiel (1 En. 20:1–7; 9:1; 40:9).

*Guardian angels:* The Bible lends to the idea that each of us may have a guardian angel assigned to us. When an angel freed Peter, he came to Mary's house (the mother of John Mark). Rhoda was excited to see Peter, but Mary thought that he was only Peter's angel (Ac. 12:15). Thus, as the text implies, guardian angels were thought to protect each person.

*Orders of angels:* Traditionally, Christians have accepted that there are at least nine orders of angels, listed from highest to lowest: seraphim, cherubim, angelic thrones, angelic dominions, angelic virtues, angelic powers, angelic principalities, archangels, and regular angels. The order of thrones consists of angels that attend to the throne of God and allow others access to the throne room. Dominions comprise angels that keep the world in order, delivering God's justice to unjust situations. Powers are often thought to be warrior angels because of the power they exercise over the agents of darkness. Virtues exercise control over the elements. Principalities are an order of angels that have command over the lower-level angels. Paul mentions most of these angelic orders in Colossians 1:16.

Here is an important truth to remember: Angels are ministering spirits that are pure, holy, and obedient to the Lord. All these angels will be seen in their glory in heaven. Society tends to view angels as powerless entities or objects of worship. A cherub is anything but a winged, chubby, baby. Some angels may not even possess wings. Angels are mighty, intense, sentinels of God's holiest places and ministering spirits who help humans draw closer to God and serve him more faithfully, but they are not to be worshiped.

Before moving on, I need to share a personal experience with you that has forever changed my outlook on angelic beings. On three separate occasions, I had encounters with what I believe were angels. The first time happened at a local hospital in Winston-Salem, NC. I was visiting a parishioner from the church I served. She had been diagnosed with terminal cancer.

She was in a room on the 8<sup>th</sup> floor of the hospital. Her blinds were closed and the only light that entered the room was from the hallway. I sat next to the window facing her bed with the door standing opposite to my position.

As we were talking, we both witnessed a dazzling body of light that came from the wall facing the foot of her bed. The body of light hovered over her bed for 15 to 30 seconds. She and I were in awe of the magnificent sight! The light from the source reflected off the walls and ceiling, indicating that whatever this body was, it was the source of the illuminating light. Oddly, though the light was incredibly bright, it neither hurt our eyes nor caused us to squint. As quickly as the being appeared, it left back through the wall from whence it came. A few seconds passed before either of us said anything. Those seconds seemed like hours. I looked around the room to see if anything could have produced that light. Yet nothing was found. Struggling to find the words to say and lacking candor at the moment, I finally blurted out, "What in the world was that?!?" The cancer-ridden saint of God looked at me, with a tear in her eye, and replied, "I am not sure." While neither of us admitted it, we both realized that we had encountered an angel.

The second occasion also happened with another witness. I was at a church function with a young lady who had cerebral palsy. She claims to have seen angels on numerous occasions. Life had not been easy on this lady. But one would never know by meeting her, as she maintained a strong heart for God. On this evening, both she and I caught a glimpse of an angel out of the corner of our eyes. It stood behind others in the fellowship building but disappeared before anyone could see it, outside of this young lady and me. The young lady smiled and said, "That was my guardian angel." While it is impossible to say with any degree of certainty who the angel was, the angel did bear a striking resemblance to the being of light that I first observed at the hospital.

My final encounter with angels—at least as of this writing—was the most personal of all. My wife and I had miscarried twice. We did not know if we would even be able to have children. So, when God blessed us with a child, we were both a bit over-protective—"a bit" is probably an understatement. With this in mind, one could understand why we were rattled when we discovered that my son would have to undergo surgery to fix a mysterious trigger thumb that he developed at the age of two. One morning at breakfast, my son said to my wife while showing her his thumb, "Mommy, it doesn't work." The surgery was a simple procedure, but it would require anesthesia. Any parent knows that surgery of any kind is major to the family undergoing it, especially when it involves a little one. I was notably frightened at the thought of my son going through surgery.

The day before my son's surgery, I stood in the hallway of our small house in Yadkinville, North Carolina while looking in my son's room. My wife was trying to explain the procedure to my son and comforted him. As I looked into his room with my wife sitting next to my son, the same recognizable light stood beside me. This time I was able to see a figure, although I could never make out the being's face. The being was around 5' 11" and had a pleasant and loving presence. The form of the being appeared to be masculine, even though that could not be deciphered. The love that emanated from the being is something that I will never forget. Even though the light did not hurt my eyes, the brilliance of the being's light was brighter than anything I had ever observed. The nature of divine light is something I had read about from people experiencing NDEs. I was able to confirm the same characteristics of divine light that they described. If my angelic experiences tell us anything about heaven, it says that heaven is going to be a place of perfect love and comfort.

## The Human Citizens (7:9–10)

Revelation 7:9–10 paints a marvelous picture of the people in heaven. John writes the following:

> After this I looked, and there was a vast multitude from every nation, tribe, people, and language, which no one could number, standing before the throne and before the Lamb. They were clothed in white robes with palm branches in their hands. And they cried out in a loud voice: Salvation belongs to our God, who is seated on the throne, and to the Lamb! (Rev. 7:9–10).

The text in Revelation answers many questions about the people who are found in heaven.

First, how many people will be in heaven? Some groups claim that only 144,000 will be in heaven, but is this true? Revelation tells us that there will be 144,000 people saved during the time of the global tribulation, a time when God judges the world (Rev. 14:1ff). Some scholars posit that 144,000 is a metaphorical number that represents believers of all time and, therefore, is not to be taken literally.[2] There is a great deal of merit to this position as 144,000 is a square of 12 multiplied by 1,000. The number 12 is often identified with governance and the people of God. Even if this position is accurate, it does not necessitate that one takes the number literally and holds that only 144,000 people will be in heaven. Revelation 7:9–10 discredits that position as the phrase "vast multitude" (Gk. *ochlos polus*) denotes a number greater than the numerical range allowed by the ancient writers. That is, the number was too large to count. Another possibility is that these 144,000 are saints who perish in the great tribulation[3] and meet with those already in heaven in Rev. 7:9–10. Nonetheless, the ultimate number of people in heaven is simply innumerable.

Second, what nationalities will be represented in heaven? Racism has plagued the history of the United States of America. Since early colonial times, certain groups of people were viewed as less valuable than others. Sometimes the level of racism reached the point that people of darker skin were viewed as subhuman. As an example, slaveholding southern Christians held the notion that the curse of Ham was that he had dark skin (Gen. 9:22–29). This is quite a bizarre assessment seeing that Jesus himself had darker olive-toned skin.

Unfortunately, racism is not quarantined to one locale. Rather, it is found in nearly every nation and culture. A typical "us versus them" mind-set develops. In stark contrast to the racist notions that some people have possessed, heaven is depicted as a place where the saints of God emerge from every "nation, tribe, people, and language" (7:9). Everyone will be able to understand each other. And there will not be even the semblance of racist ideologies in heaven. Why? For one, all the saints were clothed with white robes with palm branches in hand (7:9). The white robes indicate their purity in heaven and the palm branches describe their adoration of God and his Lamb. This leads the heavenly multitude to sing together proclaiming that salvation belongs to God and his Messiah (7:10). Also, people from different times will be in heaven. Have you ever wanted to meet people of the past? If they received Christ, you will be able to talk with them in heaven. You won't be rushed. You can take time to talk with people from history and even your ancestors. Who knows? Perhaps Moses will lead seminars describing what he learned about God and his faith when

---

2. This is the position taken by Craig Keener. See Keener, *Revelation*, 370. See also Beale, *Book of Revelation*, 416.

3. Rydelnik and Vanlaningham, *Moody Bible Commentary*, 2010.

he stood against Pharaoh. Maybe he will discuss the awe of God's presence that he experienced on Mt. Sinai. When serving in pastoral ministry, I used to walk in the cemeteries of the churches I served, looking at the tombstones. I often thought to myself how interesting it would be to talk with those of the church who passed away in the 1800s. One day, we will. Time will not hinder our ability to converse with people from all time periods.

## The Animal Citizens (Isa. 11:1–9)

Going back to my conversation with Sandy, Sandy was an animal lover. She owned several dogs, but her last pet was named Sassy.[4] Sassy provided Sandy with companionship for many years. Sassy was a cute, cuddly, tan, and silver-colored Yorkie. If you know anything about Yorkies, you know that they are compassionate little dogs. Sandy would take Sassy with her nearly everywhere she went. This included times when she took Sassy to her daughter's house for playtime adventures. Sandy's daughter-in-law shared a picture of Sandy with her dog in hand while sporting the biggest smile that one could ever wear.

It is easy to know why Sandy became emotional as she struggled to ask her next question knowing how attached she had become to her animal friends. With her voice crackling and struggling to hold back her tears, she inquired, "Preacher, this may sound funny, or maybe even foolish to many. But I have had many wonderful dogs throughout my life. Even now, I have a dog that has become like family to me. Do you think God would let me see my dogs in heaven? I cannot even imagine heaven without them."

Sandy's question was far from foolish. Dogs have provided great help to those suffering from PTSD and other ailments. Furthermore, I took a poll of the most asked questions about heaven. The most frequently asked question of all was whether animals would be found in heaven. Some may scoff at such a question. But I think it is a completely legitimate thing to ask. Animals are God's creations. So, why would not a spot that is fancied to be the greatest conceivable place not feature something beneficial to so many people?

To answer Sandy's question, I described the picture that Isaiah gave in Isaiah 11:1–16. Isaiah chapter 11 returns to the theme of a messianic

---

4. A big thanks goes out to Ashley Bennett Groce and Felicia Bennett Riddle who provided additional information about Sandy's dog Sassy.

hope which was previously noted in chapters 7 and 9.[5] In chapter 11, Isaiah describes a new kingdom ruled by the Messiah. One of the biggest push-backs that I have received in using this text for the new creation is that the pictures may describe the thousand-year Millennial Reign of Christ.

I do not think that this objection holds much weight for two reasons. First, the phrase "on that day" is eschatological in scope contrasting the Exodus, when a remnant returned to the promised land, with the new messianic kingdom where people from all nations will come together under the banner of Christ.[6] While the Millennial Kingdom of Christ is also eschatological, it is understood by dispensationalists to only be temporary. Isaiah tends to indicate greater permanency. Second, even if Isaiah 11 does depict the Millennial Kingdom, would we expect the new creation to be lesser than the temporary Millennial reign? The new creation is anticipated to be the greatest of all possible scenarios. Thus, could we expect the blessings of the Millennial Reign to be absent from the new creation? I think not. This new kingdom is a living kingdom, vibrant with life and splendor. Not only does this kingdom have animals, but it also exudes effervescent life of all kinds!

This kingdom would arise from a "shoot [growing] from the stump of Jesse" (Isa. 11:1). What is meant by that? In the OT, judgment is often associated with the cutting down of a tree. The person receiving judgment is compared to a tree, whereas the lumberjack is viewed as God. When we built our house, a large leaning pine tree was found in the back of our property. The tree was not a beautiful tree by any stretch of the imagination, but we liked it. The pine became almost iconic at dusk as its branches would shine in the glowing sunset. The branches of the tree leaned as if to say, "Welcome home!" My wife named the tree "The Sunset Crazy Tree" because of the dichotomy of its ugliness in the daytime and its beauty at sunset. We moved into our new home in July 2020. Disaster struck in late October as our area suffered from the remnants of Hurricane Zeta. Strong winds and torrential rains were too much for the poor tree. Our beloved Sunset Crazy Tree fell. As we had to cut down its remains, it became apparent that the tree had been diseased for quite some time. Despite its over 50-year life, Sunset Crazy Tree was eventually going to fall.

The OT writers recognized that their civilization was sick, and the Davidic line would soon be cut down. Despite its destruction, God promised a new sprout would emerge to breathe life back into the promises given

5. Rydelnik and Vanlaningham, *Moody Bible Commentary*, 1026.
6. Barker and Kohlenberger, *Expositor's Bible Commentary*, 1065.

to David, promises of an everlasting kingdom. The Messiah would be the fulfillment of that promise. Two insights are brought to light in Isaiah's imagery of a messianic sprout.

First, the new kingdom would be built upon the history of God's people. God would not forget his people. He will not forget about David despite the issues of the times. He will not forget about the wonderful things done in his name. You have probably heard it said that you cannot carry anything with you in eternity. Well, that is not completely true. You carry with you God's blessings for all eternity.

Second, the promises of God will never be forgotten. God will fulfill every promise he has ever given. The troubles found in the old covenants had nothing to do with God's faithfulness to the covenant agreement. Rather, the trouble was found in human faithfulness. Humans kept breaking their end of the bargain. That is why a new covenant was required. The new covenant would involve God doing everything sufficient for human salvation. In the new Messianic kingdom, all of God's promises will be fulfilled.

I recall reading a story of a pastor who visited an elderly gentleman. The gentleman was sad not because of the disease which would take him out of this world, but rather because the man of faith could not remember certain passages of Scripture. The pastor asked, "Why does this bother you so badly?" The senior replied, "These passages contained the promises that God has given me. I am sad because I cannot remember the promises of God." The wise pastor retorted, "Do you think God has forgotten them?" The old man smiled and noted, "I guess you're right." The weakened gentleman rested easy even as he passed into eternity because he trusted in God's faithfulness.

Some may wonder why Isaiah needed to recall the history of the Davidic line. This may be answered by the popularity of services like Ancestry. com and 23 and Me. Genealogies and DNA tests have become popularized as people desire to know where they originated. The classic adage states, "Those who cannot remember the past are doomed to repeat it."[7] In Jesus's heavenly kingdom, the blessings and promises of the past are fully actualized in the reality of his new living kingdom. This kingdom would come from One upon whom the Spirit of the Lord rested (Isa. 11:2). He will govern his kingdom justly and righteously (Isa. 11:2–5). Because of his righteous leadership, peace will be found in God's kingdom. This harmony extends over God's creation.

7. This statement is attributed to George Santayana.

Regarding the new creation, there will be animal life. Notice in verses 6–8 that the prophet depicts a time when animals will live in perfect harmony with humanity and each other. Though many think the Bible speaks of the lion lying down with the lamb, it says "wolf and the lamb" (Isa. 11:6). Predator and prey live in perfect harmony. The cow and bear will graze together with their calves and cubs (Isa. 11:7). Children will be able to play with even the most poisonous and lethal of animals and will not be harmed (Isa. 11:8). Not only will the new creation feature animal life, but all animals will also be tame. Humanity will live in perfect harmony with creation. There will be no curse on the land. I cannot help but think that there will be no need or place for animals like mosquitoes in heaven. If they did exist, they would not bite humans or animals. With this creation, God called it good (Gen. 1), but with the new heaven, he will call it great! Animals are a blessing to many people on earth. I have worked with people in hospice ministry who bring emotional support animals to visit with patients. It is amazing to see how dogs and even cats recognize the needs of those who are sick and ailing. Animals are blessings of God.

I recall an episode of the Twilight Zone where a man and his dog pass away on a hunting trip. The devil tries to trick the man into coming into hell with him but said that he must leave his dog outside the fence. The man refused and said, "What type of a place would heaven be if a man couldn't bring his faithful dog?" Luckily for the man and his dog, they avoided the first gate and journeyed to a second gate where an angel in overalls welcomed both the man and his dog. While this story includes a lot of fanciful thinking, I do think it hits on an important point. Animals have played an important role in the lives of many on earth. If God is that than which nothing greater could be conceived and his heaven is a place than which nothing greater could be conceived, then it only stands to reason that heaven will contain all the sanctified things that we enjoy on this earth but on a much grander scale. In my honest estimation, I believe that heaven will contain animals because I believe that heaven is a place of abundant life. Since God produces life, God could certainly allow our pets to be with us for all eternity, even if it involves recreating them.

## The Scene of the City (21:9–14, 22–27; 22:1–5)

In chapters 21 and 22 of Revelation, we catch a glimpse of what the heavenly city in the new creation will look like. Three attributes of the city are especially seen in these chapters. First, the city's connection with Christ is shown. Second, the city's holiness is demonstrated by the citizens found within. Finally, the life of the city is shown to relate to its source: God.

## The City's Connection (21:9–23)

As we have noted, if God is that than which nothing greater can be conceived, then heaven—the ultimate gift God gives humanity—will be a place than which nothing greater can be conceived. The city itself is connected to God through his Son Jesus. This becomes true as John surveils the land with the guidance of the angel in Revelation. Previously, an angel had shown John seven bowls of God's wrath that were poured out upon the earth at the end of the world (21:9). This angel called John up to where he was. The angel carried John away in the Spirit to a high mountain where he showed John the holy city of God that was to come (21:10). High mountains have often been associated with the presence of the divine. For instance, Jesus took his disciples to a "high mountain" (Matt. 17:1) where he would be transfigured. God met Moses on Mount Sinai, a high mountain in its own right.[8] On this holy mountain, John would see the New Jerusalem—the capital of the New Creation.

The gates of New Jerusalem are arrayed with every precious stone imaginable, all luminescent with a wide array of colors. The number 12 refers to the Twelve Disciples and the twelve tribes of Israel. The foundation of the city was adorned with twelve gemstones, which were derived from the priest's breastplate (Exod. 28:17–20). As we go through these stones, keep in mind that the identification of these stones and the color associated with them is not always known with certainty. Jasper was the first stone. Red is the most common color for the stone, but it has been known to be yellow, brown, green, and in the rarest of cases, blue. In Chapter 4, we previously mentioned the reasons for believing that the color blue was the likely color in mind, although we cannot know for sure. Jasper could be a diamond. It is a stone that is often associated with God's glory, such as in Revelation 4:3.[9] Regardless of the hue, jasper is associated with God's holiness.

---

8. If Jabal Mousa is the authentic Mount Sinai, then it stands at an amazing 7,497 feet. Mount Hermon, the possible mountain upon which Jesus was transfigured, stands at a whopping 9,232 feet.

9. Beale, *Book of Revelation*, 1080.

The second stone was a sapphire which is a dark blue color. The sapphire here may refer to lapis lazuli, a dark blue color associated with God and his throne. Further strengthening the case for the stone being identified with lapis lazuli is its identification with the second row of gemstones of the priest's breastplate.[10]

The third is a siliceous stone called chalcedony, which is often a pale blue color (often grayish blue) but can come in other varieties. The fourth stone is a deep green gem known as the emerald. The fifth is sardonyx, a precious stone that comes in the colors red, white, black, and gray. The sixth stone is carnelian. Carnelian ranges from a pale red, resembling a peach, to a darker hue of red. A native of the East Indies, the gemstone was often used for rings and seals.

The seventh stone is chrysolite. Many gemologists are uncertain of the precise identification of chrysolite. However, our modern topaz presumably most closely aligns with the ancient chrysolite. If their assessment holds, then the stone would be almost lime green in appearance.

The eighth stone is beryl. Beryl comes in three varieties: morganite (a peachy color), aquamarine (turquoise), and emerald (green). While it is impossible to know with certainty which variety of beryl that John saw, I tend to think it may have been the aquamarine version seeing that turquoise was listed as one of the gemstones on the high priest's breastplate.

Topaz represents the ninth stone. Topaz is linked with the previously mentioned chrysolite. However, it appears that the two find some degree of distinction. Certain versions of topaz may be bright yellow, wine-colored, and pale blue. Most interesting is that this gemstone can become electrified when rubbed or heated. Biblical topaz most likely was of a bright yellow hue.

The tenth stone is chrysoprase. Chrysoprase could represent the agate of the priest's breastplate. Chrysoprase is a bright green gemstone that is composed of silica and nickel to a smaller degree. Because of its composition, the green of chrysoprase may have been akin to the apple green hue.

Jacinth is the eleventh stone. It may also be called hyacinth. The jacinth stone was probably linked with the color of the hyacinth flower which ranged from hues of red to bright orange. Either way, the stone most likely represents the orange color of the spectrum.

---

10. "The first row was a row of carnelian, topaz, and emerald; the second row, a turquoise, a lapis lazuli, and a diamond; the third row, a jacinth, an agate, and an amethyst; and the fourth row, a beryl, an onyx, and a jasper" (Exod. 39:10b–13).

The twelfth and last stone mentioned is amethyst. Amethyst is of a dark purple hue. Sometimes the stone can be colorless, resembling the modern-day diamond. Nonetheless, the stone is of the utmost beauty. As one can see, every color of the rainbow is represented in the twelve stones of the New Jerusalem. Heaven will be anything but drab and boring. Rather, the heavenly walls contain every color imaginable. Imagine these colorful gemstones sparkling in the effervescent glory of God.

But more important than the luscious beauty of heaven, verses 22–23 states that no temple is to be found in the city because God and the Lamb fill the city with their presence. The city itself is a new temple. God's glory fills the place with his love, grace, and holiness. The gemstones, the walls, and the new creation itself radiate the Shekinah glory of God—the glory that only one high priest was able to encounter on one day each year. This glory will be readily available to any and everyone who steps foot in the new creation. Furthermore, nothing will be able to separate a person from God's loving presence.

Some have taken the street of gold and the other gemstones to be nothing more than symbolism. Such a viewpoint is warranted due to the great deal of symbolism employed in the passage. For instance, the number 12 represents a perfect government. Therefore, the writer may be pointing the reader to God's perfect government in New Jerusalem. Likewise, the twelve stones are directly linked with the high priest's breastplate, noting God's holiness and possibly the individual priesthood of each believer as set apart by Christ. However, I do not think that these details need to be symbolic only. God often reminds people in the New Testament of the ways that he came through for them in Old Testament times. God's works in history stand as place markers to remind the faithful of the ways that he has helped them in the past, in order to empower their faith to accomplish great things for him in the present and future. Likewise, the walls of the city may very well be established in such a way as to remind the citizens of heaven of the ways that God's love was exhibited for them throughout their time on earth.

Whether you hold the city's description in Revelation to be literal or symbolic, the most important truth found in Revelation is that it is going to be beautiful. The thing that makes heaven so beautiful is the connection it has with God. To be in God's glory is to experience the greatest of beauty, peace, and joy.

## The City's Holiness (21:24–27)

Just as God's glory is connected to the holy city, John shows that the city does not need any sunlight because God's holy radiance shines through it (21:24–23). The city radiates with God's holiness so that only those who walk by his light will walk in its gates (21:24). The city's gates never close because there is no danger outside the gates (21:25). Furthermore, nothing unclean will ever enter the gates noting that all evil has been quarantined in hell (21:26–27).

Heaven will be a holy place that will radiate with God's glory. His holiness will shine and radiate throughout his heavenly abode. The Bible describes God's holiness as something that is passed on from God to other people and/or things. Because the believer has received salvation, he or she has received God's holiness. However, life often keeps us from experiencing the fullness of God's holiness and glory. In contrast, heaven is a place replete with God's holiness.

While governments and political leaders often act in corrupt and even evil ways, heaven will be a place of sheer holiness. No evil will ever enter therein because God's glory shines through heaven in a penetrating fashion. In recent years, we have been bombarded with news of school shootings. I live near Mount Airy, North Carolina. Mount Airy is better known as its fictional counterpart Mayberry RFD, popularized by the famed comedy series the Andy Griffith Show. Many have moved to Mount Airy to capture what they perceive to be the idyllic nature of the fictional town, including the late Betty Lynn, the actress who played Thelma Lou on the Andy Griffith Show. Unfortunately, Mount Airy does not always live up to its fictional counterpart. Shootings, road rage, and theft have occurred in Mount Airy. Yes, crime does happen in Mayberry! When I reported some of the things that happened on social media, people were aghast to think that such a thing could happen in Mayberry. Though Mount Airy is a lovely place, it is far from heaven. In heaven, police departments, funeral homes, and hospitals will all be out of business. There will be no need for hospice workers as there will be no more death. Heaven will be the only place where we will experience what it is like to be completely crime free!

## The City's Life (22:1–5)

What will life be like in a place imbued with the glory of God? In chapter 22, the city is described vibrantly. First, John sees a river of life flowing from the throne of God and the Lamb (22:1). The river flows through the middle of the city. From the river, life abounds. Because of the life flowing from the tree of life, no curse or disease will be found in the city.

The new creation will be completely different than the modern one with even new laws of physics. One of the fundamental laws of physics is the second law of thermodynamics. The law states that the more energy is transferred or transformed, the more that it is wasted. Thus, the state of entropy increases. Entropy is a quality that describes the unavailability of energy. In other words, entropy is a state of disorder and decay. Consider our bodies. The state of decay is linked with entropy. Ultimate entropy comes from death. Thus, the physical state of this universe leads to death, disorder, and decay. But this is not the case in the new creation, extropy rather than entropy rules the day.[11] Life rather than decay increases in the heavenly abode. Because everything God touches abounds with life and vitality, life will flourish and will continue for all eternity. A person's health will not decrease over time as it does in the present cosmos. Rather, the exact opposite ensues. A person's health only gets better the longer one is in heaven. Each passing day presents new experiences, new encounters, and new abilities as one grows in the grace and glory of God.

The state of extropy may sound like something from a sci-fi film, but this is simply not the case when one examines the nature of God in the pages of Scripture. From the first pages of Genesis, God speaks, and life abounds (Gen. 1:1; see also Jn. 1:1–5). The healing ministry of Jesus personifies the life-abounding touch of the Almighty. Even with the sound of his voice, Jesus was able to bring healing to a centurion's servant (Matt. 8:5–13; Lk. 7:1–10). Likewise, the tree of life and the nourishing river of life both exude life to anything and everything it touches. They are both filled with the life-abundant extropic power of God. Astrophysicist Hugh Ross argued that "Logic dictates that if a superior life awaits—an existence above and beyond this earthly reality—the world as we know it must be inferior,

---

11. The term *entropy* comes from two Greek terms: *en* meaning "in" and *trophos* meaning "transformation." Thus, entropy describes an inner transformation of decay. In contrast, *extropy* comes from two Greek terms: *ex* "out" and *trophos* also meaning "transformation." Thus, extropy describes a transformation that comes the internal system has on its environment.

imperfect."[12] That is, it only stands to reason that the new creation will be even better than the present creation. Furthermore, it also stands to reason that the new creation will hold a completely different and exponentially better set of physics than the present world contains.

There is no example, to my knowledge, of an extropic system in our universe. God stands alone as an extropic being. Thomas Aquinas understood that God existed as pure act. He writes, "Therefore it is that the Essence of God, the pure and perfect act, is simply and perfectly in itself intelligible; and hence God by His own Essence knows Himself, and all other things also."[13] In this case, Aquinas argues that only God knows himself perfectly. However, Aquinas uses the concept of God's existence as pure act to point out several other aspects of God in his *Summa Theologica*.

For the present purposes, it is important to understand the distinction Aquinas draws between God existing as pure act as opposed to all other beings existing as both act and potency. Just as God is the only Being that can exist as pure act, so it is that only God can exist as pure extropy—an eternal, life-giving, life-sustaining, eternal Being. As such, since God exists as that than which nothing greater can be conceived, along with his existence as pure act and pure extropy, then it is implicated that heaven will be not only a place than which nothing greater can be conceived, but it will also exist in a pure eternal and extropic state.

Therefore, the new creation will find a startling new law of physics governing life as it is imbued with the divine presence of Almighty God. Rather than decay increasing, life increases! Rather than the conditions worsening, life only gets better the longer you are in heaven. With this being the case, it could be anticipated that each day in heaven is better than the previous one. Day 1 in heaven will be great, but Day 2 will be better than Day 1. Day 3 will be better than Day 2, Day 4 will be better than Day 3, and so on to *ad infinitum*. Only God has the capacity to improve on perfection.

Second, the throne of God is shown to be in the city as there is no separation between God and humanity any longer (22:3–4a). Craig Keener observes that "the lack of a temple in the new Jerusalem (21:22) contrasts starkly with traditional Jewish expectations of the end time, in which a new temple was the central feature of the city. A prayer in the regularly recited Eighteen Benedictions looked for a renewal of the temple, as did other

---

12. Ross, *Hidden Treasures in the Book of Job*, 192.

13. Aquinas, *Summa Theologica* 1.q87.a1.

Jewish sources."[14] Yet Paul and others understood that the "God who made the world and everything in it—he is Lord of heaven and earth—does not live in shrines made by hands" (Acts 17:24). The temple was not as much of a place that housed God as it was a place where people came to interact with God. In this new creation, a temple is not needed because the entire creation is God's temple! Everyone in heaven has direct and open access to the Creator! People are said to have the name of God imprinted on their foreheads. I don't take this to be literal, but rather symbolic of the interpersonal relationship that God has with his people. As such, God is ours, and we are God's. Nothing can interfere with that relationship.

Third, there is no need for the sun and the moon any longer because God's glory radiates throughout the new creation which gives the new creation all the warmth it needs for vegetation. Does this mean that there are no other planets and the like? I don't think so. The New Jerusalem is the capital city of the new creation. Thus, just as creation surpasses the physical Jerusalem on earth, so the new heavens and the new earth will be much larger than the capital city alone. Rather, I think it shows that in the New Jerusalem, God's light shines throughout the city and penetrates every part of the new creation.

Even though God's spiritual presence is found in every corner of this universe, his Shekinah glory (i.e., personal presence) is not due to the penalty of human sin. For instance, God's omnipresence tells us that God is everywhere. But that does not entail that God has a personal relationship with every being in creation. Up until the time of the new covenant, only the high priest could access the Shekinah glory of God in the inner sanctum on Yom Kippur. Now, the Shekinah glory is available to all who enter the new covenant with God through Christ. The Shekinah glory is accessed through the Holy Spirit of God. In the new creation, both God's Shekinah glory and spiritual presence are found unhindered.

The new creation of God will be one that will be beaming with life. Death will no longer separate us. We will never be separated from our loved ones again. Disease will no longer separate us. We will never be weakened by the aging process, nor will we ever worry about contamination. Sin will no longer separate us. Our relationship with God will never be severed and neither will we suffer separation from our human relationships due to misunderstandings. While we suffer disease, depression, and despair, we will no longer worry about those things in heaven. Let us seek to reconcile our

14. Keener, *Revelation*, 497.

relationship with God and others so that heaven will not be such a shock to our system.

Certain things give us a foretaste of heaven. As noted previously, I thoroughly enjoy a good fire in my fire pit. There is something special about the crackling of the flames that puts all my worries at ease. The same is true of the soothing ocean waves at the beach, the sound of water flowing over rocks in a fresh mountain stream, or the rustling of the leaves in a summer breeze. Perhaps your form of relaxation is found in something else. Regardless, these practices are a mere foretaste of the peace and serenity that we will experience in heaven. When we get a taste of such relaxation, we don't want to come back to the "real world." But what if the real world was the state in which we find ourselves in such relaxing moments? That will be the case in heaven.

## Conclusion

As Sandy and I went through this content, her anxieties continued to calm, and her wall of defense began to lower. She began to understand the love that God had for her far exceeded anything that she could have envisioned. Sandy is far from the only one. I am still haunted by an interaction that I had with another lady who told me after I had read Romans 8:35–39, that she neither knew that God loved her so deeply nor did she realize that the Bible said such things. For Sandy, she was beginning to realize that God was not the harsh judgmental ogre that some religious parishioners had depicted him to be. Rather, God was a loving heavenly Father that only wanted the best for her. Unfortunately, many people never come to grasp the depth of God's love before crossing the threshold of death. I am glad I could serve as God's mouthpiece during this interaction.

Concerning the question on the table, heaven is a place where angelic and human citizens will live in perfect harmony. It is a place where God will eliminate all disease and death and where we will live with God in perfect harmony. We often get distracted by the images of heaven. We think upon the streets of gold and the walls of jasper so much that we fail to realize that what makes heaven so heavenly is God's involvement with it. God is the most beautiful being or thing that you will ever see. Thus, it only makes sense that his heaven is filled with boundless beauty and luminous life.

*Chapter Six*

---

# WILL WE KNOW ONE
# ANOTHER IN HEAVEN?

*Matthew 17:1–13*

1. Background of the Transfiguration

2. The Prophets' Identities were Known (17:3, 4–8, 11)

   a. *Known by God/Jesus*

   b. *Known by Disciples*

3. The Prophets' Relationships were Known (17:1–3)

   a. *With each Other (17:1)*

   b. *With God (17:2–3)*

4. The Prophets' Positions were Known (17:4, 11–13)

   a. *By Jesus (17:11–13)*

   b. *By Disciples (17:4)*

A N HOUR HAD PASSED with my telephone conversation with Sandy. Previously, I had been pacing back and forth in front of the church's altar with a bit of anxiety as I hoped I was answering Sandy's questions appropriately. I had been sitting for a while. But now, it was time to get a bit more comfortable. The Lord had given me a sense of peace as I spoke with Sandy, something I felt coming from her as well. The longer we spoke on the issues of heaven, the more peace God gave both of us. So, I decided to answer any remaining questions with full comfort. With my feet propped up and leaning back in the pew as if it were a recliner, I prepared myself for any additional questions she may have held.

Sandy had suffered quite a bit of loss in her life. Her husband Gwyn had died and left her a widow. As badly as she was hurt by the death of her husband, it was the loss of her two sons that bothered her the most. Why would God take her children? This is troubling for any parent, as the normal pattern is for the child to outlive his or her parents. Having lost two children by miscarriage, I understand the pain associated with the loss of one's child. However, the grief associated with such a loss is increased exponentially when the parent comes to know and loves the child face-to-face. While my wife and I were hurt greatly over the loss of our children in the womb, I know that parents who lost their children who were children, teenagers, or even adults must experience the greatest pain that anyone could ever imagine. So, I entered this topic with the greatest of sensitivities, knowing the burden Sandy carried with this topic.

Sandy, choking back her tears, asked, "Preacher, I have to know. Will I know my family and friends in heaven? Will I know my family who has passed before me?" Sandy's question is one asked by many. Unlike the previous questions, the answer to this question is not found in the apocalyptic or eschatological literature of the Bible. Rather, the answer is found in a bizarre occurrence in the life of Jesus. To this, we go to a mysterious encounter that Jesus had with the disciples, an event known as the Transfiguration.

## Background of the Transfiguration

Jesus and the disciples had just been in Caesarea Philippi. The town was known as the ancient Las Vegas of the time. It was known for its excesses and had something comparable to a red-light district near the mouth of what many held to be an opening to hell. At the mouth of what was perceived to be the entrance to hell, Jesus proclaimed victory over the powers of darkness after Simon Peter professed that Jesus was the "Messiah, the Son of the living God" (Matt. 17:16). The cave features what appears to be a bottomless pit. Locals constructed idols to pay homage to the Greek god Pan, the god of the wilderness. The gateway to hell was situated at the base of Mount Hermon, one of the tallest mountains in the Levant.[1] Standing at 9,232 feet in elevation, Mount Hermon remains snowcapped throughout much of the year. The snowmelt serves as a source for the Jordan River.

Mount Hermon fits as the location for the Transfiguration for two reasons. First, Jesus and the disciples had been in Caesarea Philippi. Caesarea Philippi is only 14 miles from Mount Hermon. Contrast that with the 62-mile trek that Jesus and the disciples would have journeyed if they traveled to the traditional Mount of Transfiguration, located southwest of the Sea of Galilee. Second, the text notes that Jesus brought Peter, James, and John to a high mountain—*eis oros hupselon* (Matt. 17:1). Mount Hermon fits the bill as a very high mountain.

As they were on the mountain, Jesus was transfigured before them. The term *metamorphothe*, (i.e., "transfigured") indicates that Jesus had taken on a different form or appearance.[2] Both Moses and Elijah—two men who had encountered the divine presence of God on a mountain—stood next to Jesus. Jesus conversed with the two prophets. Though the prophets had passed many years before the disciples' birth,[3] they knew the prophets as indicated by Peter's desire to build three tabernacles, one for Jesus, one for Moses, and another for Elijah (Matt. 17:4).

This passage of Scripture helps us understand the knowledge held for each other within the scope of Jesus's transfiguration. While Jesus had not yet died and been resurrected, he was elevated to his glorified status during this period. Two deceased, yet still very much spiritually alive, prophets stood beside Jesus. Moses and Elijah were allowed to visit Jesus with their spiritual bodies. How did each person relate to another? The passage helps us understand three ways in which we know each other in eternity—we know each other's identity, relationship, and position in eternity.

## The Prophets' Identities Were Known (17:3, 4–8, 11)

A fictional story is told of a woman who hired a medium to bring back the spirit of her dead husband—or at least I hope it is fictional. The woman had been known to pester her husband quite a bit during their marriage. When the husband appeared in ghostly form, she asked, "Honey, is it better up

1. Mount Hermon is second only to Qurnat as Sawda which stands at 10,131 feet.

2. Louw-Nida, *Greek-English Lexicon of the NT,* 58.16, 586.

3. Moses died a natural death (Deut. 34:1–8), whereas Elijah was taken into heaven with a chariot of fire (2 Kgs. 2).

there than it was here with me?" The husband said, "Yes, much better. But that's not saying a lot because the other place would be better than being with you." I am sure that blessed the woman's heart. Well, not really.

When looking at the prophets in their heavenly state, it is clear that God, Jesus, and the disciples knew their identities. That is, they were known by all parties involved even though they had died many years before the event.[4] The identities of the prophets were not eliminated at death, but rather they continued in the afterlife.

## Known by God/Jesus

First, notice that God and Jesus knew the prophets. God certainly knew the prophets because he is the One who allowed them to stand before Jesus. Furthermore, Jesus obviously knew the prophets because he was conversing with them while the disciples tried to understand what was happening (17:3). Additionally, this happened after John the Baptist had been executed. The disciples were probably confused because of seeing Elijah with Jesus. They had understood that Elijah was going to return to establish God's kingdom before the end. People in antiquity held to one of two interpretations of Elijah's end-time role. The first was that Elijah had not died and would return as a "literal *redivivus* figure."[5] The second was that Elijah had died, but his eschatological role would be fulfilled by another in a figurative *redivivus* manner.[6] Jesus and the NT writers held to the latter viewpoint and argued that John the Baptist had fulfilled that role (17:11–13). In other words, John the Baptist fulfilled the eschatological ministry of Elijah as he prepared the way for the Messiah. Jesus's kingdom was the eschatological messianic kingdom prophesied by Malachi. Nonetheless, most important to the present issue on the table, Jesus knew the identities of the prophets even beyond their physical deaths.

Isn't it amazing to consider that God knows us personally? I will never forget a time in the late eighties when I met Dr. Mark Corts. Dr. Mark Corts served as the senior pastor of Calvary Baptist Church in Winston-Salem, North Carolina. Calvary was, and probably still is, one of the largest congregations in the Piedmont Triad area of North Carolina. Dr. Corts

---

4. Even if one were to argue that Elijah was transferred to heaven and did not die a normal death, that still does not remove the reality of Moses's natural death.

5. Keener, *Gospel of Matthew: SRC*, 440.

6. Keener, *Gospel of Matthew: SRC*, 440.

was a stately man. He was tall and slender with tanned skin, hair perfectly combed to the side, and donning wire-rimmed glasses, giving him the look of an esteemed congressman. Dr. Corts was a man of great intelligence, integrity, and tremendous influence. I met Dr. Corts at Fruitland Baptist Bible College in Hendersonville, NC after he gave an address to the student body. After his message, I introduced myself; we exchanged pleasantries before both going our separate ways. The next night, he spoke at Mud Creek Baptist Church, another large congregation in the mountainous confines of Hendersonville, North Carolina. As we were walking out, I shook hands with Dr. Corts, and he called me by name! A man of his importance remembered someone like me even after meetings hundreds of people at both the college and Mud Creek Baptist Church.

While it was a considerable compliment to have a man like Dr. Corts remember my name, it pales in comparison to the reality of knowing that God knows each of us by name. The God who created the heavens and the earth knows each one of us. That is truly incomprehensible, but it is true! Furthermore, that will not change in heaven. God knows us thoroughly. He knew us before we were even born (Jer. 1:4–10) and had a purpose for our lives. If God knew us before we were born, it is a certainty that he will know us when we enter eternity. Even in the book of Revelation, we are taught that our identities are known, even though we may be given a new name (Rev. 2:17). While we want to know if we will know one another in heaven, the most important Person to know us in eternity is God. As long as God knows us, nothing else matters.

## Known by the Disciples

Second, the disciples knew the identities of the prophets. Notice that the disciples wanted to build three shelters to commemorate the event—one for Jesus, one for Moses, and one for Elijah (Matt. 17:4). God does not restrain a person's knowledge of other people in eternity. Rather, regular people recognize the identity of others in heaven, even those they never met on earth.

I have often walked through graveyards and contemplated what it would be like to have conversations with those who first started the churches I had served. What would it be like to speak to the saints of God who endured the horrors of the Civil War? Recently, I looked up my ancestors on an ancestry app and found that I had far more Dutch and German ancestry than I realized. I learned about some of my ancestors who immigrated to the colonial United States to avoid the famine impacting their home in the Palatinate region of Germany. I stopped and pondered what it must have been like for my ancestors to make that journey. I found myself wanting to meet them. Eventually, the citizens of heaven will be able to speak to other saints about their experiences. Those in heaven will be able to learn about the life experiences of those who precede them and those who are their successors.

A couple of things stand out to me concerning our knowledge of each other's identities. First, we will know each other in heaven. Our identities are not lost when we go to heaven. I will be known as Brian Chilton, who served as a pastor for numerous churches, a father, a son, a husband, a researcher, a writer, and so on. I will be known, and I will know others in heaven. I will know my wife, my son, and other family members who are in heaven. Neither the identity of the prophets nor the disciples was lost during this exchange.

Second, we will somehow know those in the past. The disciples recognized Moses and Elijah. But the text does not indicate that Jesus said to them, "Peter, James, and John, meet Moses and Elijah." Instead, the disciples somehow automatically knew the identities of Moses and Elijah. Could Moses and Elijah have introduced themselves? Well, they could have. But again, there is no indication in the text that they did. So, it seems that we will not only know each other as we are known, but we will also know those of the past. Perhaps this knowledge of people from time's past comes from divine intuition, revelation, or the Spirit's communion with our spirits. We can only muster to guess. Even so, we will somehow know individuals from all moments of history.

After my grandpa and grandma's passing, I have often stopped to wonder with whom they might be speaking in heaven. The Furno family are good friends of ours. Melissa Furno's father, Dr. Burch, was an extraordinary pastor and scholar. I am sure my grandpa has had many conversations with Dr. Burch, and I am sure Grandma has spoken numerous times with Mary, Jesus's mother. Furthermore, I am sure both have spent a lot of time with Jesus himself. We will know each other in heaven. In fact, we will most likely know one another better than we do now.

# The Prophets' Relationships Were Known (17:1–3)

When we talk about relationships at this point, I am not saying that marital relationships will carry over into heaven. We have a forthcoming chapter on that issue. However, the acknowledgment of our relationships on earth will be carried over into heaven. We see this in the relationships that are in view during Jesus's transfiguration with each other and with God.

## Their Relationship with Each Other (17:1)

While the disciples were not in heaven at the time, they still had the relationship they had before the experience. In like manner, the prophets had a good relationship with each other. Have you ever noticed how much worthless time we spend worrying about who is the best? Human beings have an insatiable desire to feel as if they are the best at what they do and that they are needed. Moses and Elijah were giants in their field. Yet Moses was not arguing with Elijah about being the better prophet. Rather, both shared their focus on Jesus and the task God had for them. While the relationships are different in heaven, as we will see when we talk about the absence of marriages in heaven, we will have a better relationship with each other in heaven than we do now. In heaven, we will be perfected like Christ. Therefore, we will be able to relate to one another much better than we can now.

You have probably heard the phrase "keeping up with the Joneses." The phrase speaks to the human desire to have material things as good, if not better, than their neighbors. However, I heard a speaker once say, "Why do we worry about purchasing things we don't need, with money we don't have, to impress people we don't even like?" The question is something highly worth considering. Why do we place so much emphasis on competition?

In heaven, we will not worry about competing against others. We will not worry about always trying to be the best. We will not worry about school shootings or anything of the like. In heaven, we will love one another the way God has called us to do. Disagreements and debates will be a thing of the past. Granted, we may still try to resolve certain theological conundrums. Though we will continue to grow in our knowledge, there will be no place for nastiness in heaven as often communicated on many social media posts. Thankfully, we will no longer have Baptist business meetings. And all the saints said "Amen" to that point! Add a "Praise God" and "Hallelujah!" Whether we still have theological debates in heaven or not, people will love one another the way God intended. Misunderstandings, miscommunications, and angry tirades will be a thing of the past. Divine love will reign supreme in the hearts and lives of the heavenly citizens.

## Their Relationship with God (17:2–3)

Notice that Moses and Elijah were able to stand beside Jesus in all his glory. It appears that Jesus was some distance away from the disciples to protect them. However, Moses and Elijah stood right beside Christ. The disciples assumed a prostrate posture when encountering the divine presence in the cloud. They covered their faces because they did not know if they would be able to withstand the sight of God's glory and were incredibly terrified (Matt. 17:6). Contrast this with the posture of the prophets. While the prophets were assuredly respectful and reverent of God's presence, they were able to commune with God in a fashion that the disciples were not, at least according to their comfortability.

In like manner, we will be able to relate to God in ways that we have not before. We will be able to see God in all his glory. We will hear God's voice directly. We will see him as he is. Nothing will stand between us and God ever again. Sometimes, my mind tends to drift in times of prayer. I doubt that will happen in heaven. Our relationship with God will not only continue in heaven, but it will also be better. Sin will no longer come between us and God. Even as Christians, we can allow our old nature to creep in and hinder our relationship with God. That will no longer be an issue in heaven.

During certain times of my life, I have felt the Spirit of God come upon me in ways that left me in utter awe. In times of depression, the Spirit instills feelings of spiritual ecstasy. If you have had encounters like these, you know the spiritual joy, love, and splendor that such occurrences bring. Yet these experiences are but a foretaste of the glorious joy that we will have in our unhindered relationship with God.

## The Prophets' Positions Were Known (17:4, 11–13)

In this state, the prophets were still known for their positions on earth. Their positions had undoubtedly increased and intensified in heaven, but they were still known as two of the most important OT prophets. Their positions, like their identities and relationships, were known by both Jesus and the disciples.

## By Jesus (17:11–13)

Jesus knew these men as prophets even though Moses had died 1,439 years earlier and Elijah had died 884 years prior to their meeting on the mountain. Even still, the prophets' deeds followed them into eternity. While it is true that you cannot take your material possessions with you into heaven, your good deeds are taken with you into heaven. That is to say, what you do for Christ on earth matters in eternity. This is especially true given the biblical teaching of the Judgment Seat of Christ.

During the Judgment Seat of Christ (1 Cor. 3:10–15; 2 Cor. 5), the things we do for Christ are given to us as rewards, whereas the bad deeds we commit are burned up in the fires of God's presence. Some take issue with this teaching, implying that God's forgiveness removes the penalty for all bad things done on earth. Granted, God's forgiveness pays the sin debt for everything we do. However, that does not indicate that we are allowed to do anything as we please. Otherwise, the believer turns God's grace into a license to sin. Paul describes judgment as being one where a person's work is tested. If anyone's work survives the testing of the Lord, likened to gold, silver, and gemstones, then the person will be given a reward for their work on earth (1 Cor. 3:12, 14). In contrast, if a person's work is worthless, likened to wood, hay, and straw, then the person's work will be burned (1 Cor. 3:12, 15). The person will suffer a loss, but "he himself will be saved—but only as through fire" (1 Cor. 3:15). What is the loss suffered? Perhaps it is the knowledge that the work was not fruitful. We really cannot say with certainty. Nonetheless, believers should realize that what they do on earth holds eternal significance.

Jesus, in his Parable of the Talents, tells the story of how each of us is given a gift and ability. In the parable, each person is given various talents according to their skill set. One person is given five talents, another two, and another one depending on each person's ability (Matt. 25:15). The individuals given five and two went out to use their gifts, whereas the person who had one tucked it away (Matt. 25:20–25). The first two were celebrated and were given more in the kingdom. However, the one who did nothing with his talent was cast away (Matt. 25:30). Jesus later explains that the children of God will inherit the blessings of the kingdom prepared for them when the angels separate the saints (represented as sheep) from the wicked (represented as the goats) (Matt. 25:31–34). Later, he notes that if a believer does good work for someone on earth, then his work holds a spiritual impact, as God acknowledges his or her work (Matt. 25:35–40). A little-known point that is rarely detected is that Matthew 25:31–46 serves as an explanation and further follow-up for the Parable of the Talents. The point is that our work on earth holds spiritual ramifications, as is often acknowledged by Jesus (Matt. 25:14–30).[7] The material influences the spiritual and the spiritual impacts the physical.

From the principles learned in the Parable of the Talents, it appears that we will have jobs in heaven that are well-suited for us. These jobs will not be positions that we hate, but rather things that we enjoy. Life does not always afford us the opportunities that we would like. Often, we are forced into jobs that we do not like and are not best suited for—jobs in which we are underappreciated, underpaid, and undervalued. Furthermore, office politics in many corporations tend to elevate those craving power and esteem, even to the point of celebrating those with narcissistic tendencies.[8] In contrast, those who are introverted, meek, and mild are often overlooked.

This will not be the case with the jobs God gives us in heaven. God will mete out jobs to his people according to his good pleasure and according to what best suits each person. This is apparent for a few reasons. First, God shows no partiality and is not coerced by bribery. Paul writes, "For there is no favoritism with God" (Rom. 2:11). God is not swayed by human opinions concerning importance. For example, Paul adds, "Now from those recognized as important (what they once made no difference to me; God does not show favoritism)—they added nothing to me" (Gal. 2:6). Another Pauline text adds God's lack of favoritism to those who do right and wrong, saying, "For the wrongdoer will be paid back for whatever wrong he has done, and there is no favoritism" (Col. 3:25).

Second, God created us as his workmanship to do good works. The NT reminds us that "you are saved by grace through faith, and this is not from yourselves; it is God's gift—not from works, so that no one can boast. For we are his workmanship, created in Christ Jesus for good works, which God prepared ahead of time for us to do" (Eph. 2:8–10). The term *workmanship* is translated from the Greek word ποίημα, which depicts a divine

---

7. Michael Heiser discusses the dualist understanding of the biblical writers in his book *Unseen Realm*. Heiser notes that in the Lord's Prayer, Jesus understands that "God desires to rule over all he has created: the invisible spiritual realm and the visible earthly realm. He will have his way in both domains." Heiser, *Unseen Realm*, 38.

8. Even in church life, more than one time I have heard denominational leaders laud egotistical and narcissistic traits as good leadership. Yet this is far from the servant leadership model that Jesus exemplified and exercised.

creation, a masterpiece of sorts. If we take Jesus's teachings in the Parable of the Talents seriously, then we are left with no reason to deny that God's creative work in us applies only to the physical world. God's work in us may be fully actualized in eternity.

When serving as a chaplain, I often ask a series of questions when I first meet a patient to help me get to know them better. I ask them what they did for a living, what philosophical and/or religious beliefs they hold, and what they enjoy doing for fun. For a few people, their occupations match their interests. For many others, a great disparity is found between what they enjoy doing and what they did for a living. This separation will not be found in our heavenly occupations. Some of the best teachers were never allowed to teach. Just like some of the best singers were never given a public platform to sing. In heaven, God's existence as pure actuality will elevate our potentialities to full actualities. That is, our heavenly jobs will grant us the opportunity to flourish and excel in the areas that we enjoy. There is a saying that goes, "If you enjoy what you do, you'll never work a day in your life." The expression will be fully actualized in heaven. We will finally be able to be the person we were always made to be without any inhibitions, no discouragement, and nothing holding us back. We will flourish and bloom into the masterpieces God created us to be.

I often think of the rewards we receive as being comparable to a college graduation convocation. At such a ceremony, everyone wearing the cap and gown graduates with a degree. Their degrees may be in different fields, but they have shown that they have accomplished the program before them. Some graduates may don extra cords and medals that distinguish their academic excellence. The extra work they put into the program is noted and celebrated. But at the end of the day, everyone still graduates. Our heavenly graduation convocation is much the same. All the redeemed enter heaven. However, some have worked extra hard for the Lord, and their work will be celebrated.

You may be thinking at this juncture, "I don't know if I will have offered anything to Christ with my life." If that is the case, then guess what—*you're not dead yet!!! It's never too late to start working for Christ!!!* These rewards are not a matter of bragging. Our rewards are a means to show our appreciation to Christ for what he has done for us.

## By Disciples (17:4)

The disciples recognized the position of the prophets, as well, in verse 4. Simply put, I think we will recognize what others have done for the Lord while on earth. I have a strong inclination to believe that there will be many people who will be recognized by God for doing much more than you ever expected (such as people working behind the scenes, not wanting recognition). God will glorify them, and we will greatly appreciate the work and continued work they do. Many souls who go unnoticed by the world will be recognized by God and others in heaven.

Rest assured. You may be working for God and feel like no one ever gives you credit or that no one knows what you are doing for Christ. You may feel like your voice does not matter and that no one pays you any mind. You may feel as if you are neglected by the world and worthless. The God who sees all not only knows you by name, but he also sees the wonderful things you are doing for him. One day, everyone will know the great work you do. God will bless you for it.

## Conclusion

Asbel Petrey served as a pioneer preacher in the Cumberland Mountains of eastern Kentucky in the early 1900s. One day an author, interested in writing about Petrey's spiritual adventures, visited him for an interview. He asked during the visit, "What is the greatest single thing that has happened to you during your long ministry in the Cumberlands?" Petrey pointed to a white church that was visible on a nearby hill. He said: "Two Sundays ago, I was guest of honor at services held at that church. As we entered the building, the ushers gave each person a red rose. When the services were almost over, the pastor asked me to stand. Then he said to the members of the congregation: 'If Brother Petrey was the one responsible for your finding Christ as your Saviour, come up and pin a rose on him.'" Petrey continued, "They started coming from every part of the room. They pinned roses all over my coat, down my pants legs, all over my back. I felt like a blooming idiot. But I would not trade those roses for all the hardwood in those hills nor all the coal beneath the surface of the land and all the gold in Fort Knox!" Most Christians have never heard of Asbel Petrey. Thousands just like him have remained faithful to Jesus and his call during their lifetime.

They have focused on the command of the Great Commission to make disciples (Matt. 28:19–20). We should follow their example.[9]

So, what should we take from this chapter? I contend that four points stand out. First, we will be known as we are known on earth, although our relationships will be changed. Second, our friendships and relationships will greatly increase in heaven as we will be perfected like Christ. Third, nothing will stand between us, as there will not be anything that stands between us and God. Fourth and finally, our deeds worked for Christ on earth will carry over into eternity. Meaning, that what you do for Christ on earth has eternal ramifications, resulting in great blessings upon you. The spiritual realm impacts the physical, and the physical impacts the spiritual.

Sandy was satisfied with the answer I gave. However, she asked a follow-up question that I could not answer. She asked, "But what if we have family who did not make it to heaven? Will we know? If so, would we not mourn them not being there?" I was honest with her in that I did not readily have an answer for her. I mentioned that each person is given a choice to respond to God's grace or reject it. I am not certain if we will know if some of our loved ones refused God's grace. But if we do, I think that God will show us all the manners that he tried to reach them. Like Sandy, I also wonder about this issue. Nonetheless, I think that God will protect us emotionally and spiritually in heaven, and we will know that God is wholly good and loving.

The nature of hell is something that is outside the scope of this book. Certainly, questions concerning the conditionality and timespan of hell, in addition to the possibility of annihilationism (held by Chris Date and John Stackhouse), post-mortem repentance (held by Jerry Walls), and universal reconciliation (held by Robin Parry) have taken center stage in modern Christian academia. These questions are worthwhile endeavors and may impact how one views Sandy's follow-up question. Nonetheless, such questions must be tabled for another time.

If one holds to the freedom of the will, then it can be said that a person's acceptance and rejection of God's freely offered grace is each person's prerogative. We can only hope that our loved ones will see the light of God's love before reaching that point. Furthermore, I am more convinced than ever that God continues to reach out to a person up to the point of death.

In the meantime, this should spur us on to work for the Lord on earth while we still have the opportunity to do so. My grandmother, Mildred Sisk,

9. Lea, *Hebrews, James*, 46.

bought me a Christian t-shirt when I was a teenager. The t-shirt had one of the cleverest statements I have ever seen, which read, "Keep working for the Lord. The pay isn't much, but the retirement plan is out of this world!" The saying well wraps up our obligation to the Lord. Keep working for God. The work we do on earth has eternal consequences.

# Chapter Seven

## WILL THERE BE MARRIAGES IN HEAVEN?
### Matthew 22:23–40

1. There Are No Marriages in Heaven Because Of Angelic Likeness (22:29–30)

   a. *Angelic Likeness Indicates No Gender Roles*

   b. *Angelic Likeness Indicates No Gender Relationships*

2. There Are No Marriages in Heaven Because Of Eternal Living (22:31–33)

   a. *Eternal Living Indicates No Need for Reproduction*

   b. *Eternal Living Indicates No Need for Parenting*

3. There Are No Marriages In Heaven Because of Everlasting Love (22:34–40)

   a. *Everlasting Love Comes from Our God's Love*

   b. *Everlasting Love Comes from Our Christian Love*

S ANDY HAD SUFFERED A great deal of loss in her life. As she reflected on the afterlife, she began to contemplate the relationship she had with her late husband, Gwyn. The tone in Sandy's voice implied a deep reflection as she began to ask her next question. "Now, Preacher, let me ask you. My husband passed away a few years ago. When I pass, will we remain married in heaven as we were on earth? Does that mean that we will share a mansion in heaven? How will all that work?" I wanted to handle Sandy's question with the most exquisite sense of respect, sympathy, and sincerity while appreciating the delicate nature of her inquiry. Sandy continued by saying, "I have heard some religious groups and denominations talking about how a person will remain married to their partner for all eternity. Is this right?" Sandy was right. Certain groups do claim that the marital vows made on earth will continue into eternity. But the greater question is whether Scripture says anything on the matter.

Not just anyone provided the answer to this question. The answer came from Jesus himself! In Matthew 23, a group of Sadducees approached Jesus. They desired to trick him, as was the common practice of the religious leaders of the day when interacting with Jesus. The Sadducees posed a case where a woman married a man. The man died, and then she married his brother. He died also. She kept marrying brothers after each subsequent death until she married the seventh brother. The seventh brother died as well as did the woman herself. The Sadducees asked which of the brothers would be her husband in heaven. In my mind, the greater question is this: How dumb was the seventh brother to marry this woman after watching his previous six brothers die? After a while, one would think that people would learn, but the elevator must not have gone all the way upstairs for the seventh brother.

This gives credence to the joke often told of a man who died and went to heaven. The man greets God and inquires if he can ask a few questions. God said, "Sure. Go right ahead." The man asked, "Why did you make women so pretty?" God answered, "So you would like them." The man asked his second question, "But why did you make them so beautiful?" God answered, "So you would love them." This led to the man's third and somewhat offensive question. "But God," the man continued, "why did you make some of them so ditzy?" God replied, "So some of them would love you."

In response to the Sadducees, Jesus provided a concrete answer on the topic.[1] While some groups would say, yes, people are married in heaven; Jesus concretely said, no. Jesus disclosed several major theological issues with the Sadducees' concept of the afterlife while answering their challenge (i.e., marriage in heaven, proof of the resurrection, evidence for angels, and

---

1. It may be, as Morris contends, that the Sadducees had deceived themselves on the issue of the resurrection. See Morris, *Gospel According to Matthew*, 560.

evidence for a spiritual afterlife). Jesus asserted three reasons why marriages do not exist in heaven. Let us now peer into these reasons as we move forward.

## There Are No Marriages in Heaven Because of Angelic Likeness (22:29–30)

First, Jesus notes that people do not marry in heaven because of their likeness to angels. It must be asserted that human beings do not become angels. On more than one occasion, I have heard individuals saying that their dearly departed loved ones had become angels in heaven. Yet Jesus did not say that people would become angels in the resurrection but are rather "like angels in heaven" (22:29). One must ask, what is meant by *angelic likeness*? That is the million-dollar question. Jesus bases his argument on a common understanding in classic Judaism. In the Talmud, humans are compared to angels in three ways—they have intelligence, they walk upright, and speak in a holy tongue.[2] Yet in three separate ways, humans resemble the animal kingdom—they eat and drink, they reproduce, and they defecate and urinate.[3] Thus, according to Judaism, angelic likeness includes existing as a sentient being, walking upright, and having the ability to praise God. However, angelic likeness does not include eating and drinking, reproduction, and using the bathroom. When Jesus speaks of an angelic likeness, it appears that his description contains two components: a lack of gender roles and an absence of gender-based relationships.

### Angelic Likeness Indicates No Gender Roles

First, angelic likeness indicates that people both in heaven and in the resurrection have no gender roles. This means that the binary male/female paradigm no longer exists in the afterlife. The role of gender has become a major talking point in popular society. Questions plague our modern discourse. Are men and women equal in all aspects? Are fathers and mothers equal in the marital relationship? What roles can women hold in church ministry?

These discussions offer a great deal of debate between people of the opposite sex. Even when families adopt traditional roles, there can be a

2. *b. Hagigah* 16a.
3. *b. Hagigah* 16a.

great deal of misunderstanding between parties. The classic television hit *The Andy Griffith Show* featured an episode where Sherriff Andy Taylor—the lead character of the program—speaks to his son about the distinctions between men and women. Opie, Andy's son, pipes up and says, "Pa, I don't understand women." Andy responds, "Don't worry, son, you won't understand them when you're grown either." Women reading this book will probably agree that they also do not always understand men. I am a man, and I do not always understand my fellow men. I do not understand why men in northwestern North Carolina insist on driving huge, gas-guzzling trucks when they live in a city and do not work on a farm. What is the point?

While the questions listed above are important and deserved to be discussed, Jesus seems to imply that these issues will be resolved in heaven and the resurrection as human beings will no longer require the roles of gender. Two points are implied from Jesus's didactic. First, we must confess, there are biological differences between men and women. By this, I am not touching on issues of sexuality, but rather the biological functions of reproduction.[4] That is, the male sperm unites with the female egg and creates life in the female's womb during sexual intercourse. Because biological distinctions are present, the two genders find some degree of separation. However, since Jesus implies that reproduction does not occur in the afterlife, then these biological distinctions are no longer necessary, which leads to another important implication.

Second, hostilities and confusion have sometimes existed between the sexes. As noted by the scene from the *Andy Griffith Show*, men do not always understand women, and women do not always understand men. Part of the problem is found in the curse noted in Genesis 3:16. The curse of the sin committed in the Garden included the intensification of labor pains, and that the woman's "desire will be for your husband, yet he will rule over you." The Hebrew term *mashal* describes someone holding power over someone or something, or "to have dominion."[5] But was this God's desire or was it a natural outflow of the burden that Adam and Eve brought upon themselves and humanity? It appears that the latter may be the case.

The curse spelled out in Genesis 3:16 has brought plenty of problems for women throughout history. As Millard Erickson noted, "Women have at times been regarded as, at best, second-class members of the human

---

4. The issues of sexuality are important. But as it stands, a full discussion on the issue lies beyond the scope of this present work.

5. Strong, *Enhanced Strong's Lexicon.*

race."[6] This includes everything from being forbidden to vote, holding certain jobs, and unfairly receiving less pay. In some cultures, women were viewed as their husband's property.[7]

However, Jesus held a much higher view of women, as seen in numerous examples. First, Jesus spoke to women in public settings while most rabbis avoided women (Jn. 4). Second, Jesus accepted Mary at the same level as male disciples, to the disdain of her sister Martha (Lk. 10:38–42). Third, Jesus used a woman as an evangelist for her town (Jn. 4:28–30). Finally, Jesus chose to first disclose the truth of his resurrection to the female disciples (Matt. 28:1–10). These examples are but a few that could be noted.

Even today, the role of women is a topic of hot debate. Four camps have developed over time regarding the role of women in the church. Complementarians hold that there is a strong distinction between the sexes. Two camps have emerged from this viewpoint. Strong complementarians contend that women can never exercise any leadership position over a man. Those holding this position may find themselves at odds with their places of employment since women are now CEOs, CFOs, and COOs. Soft complementarianism is the lighter version of the camp. Soft complementarians assert that women can hold any leadership position except for the role of pastor.[8]

On the other side of the spectrum is the egalitarian theological viewpoint. Egalitarians, like their complementarian counterparts, are also divided into two camps. Soft egalitarians hold that there are some biological distinctions between men and women, but they also accept the equality of both men and women as children of God. Therefore, soft egalitarians aver that both men and women can serve in any role and capacity. Strong egalitarians take the argument a step further by arguing that there are no distinctions between men and women in any capacity.

No matter which camp you find yourself in, the final result of heaven will lend itself to an absolute clearance of any and all curses. As such, heaven produces an environment in which there are no distinctions between men and women. As Paul noted, "There is no Jew or Greek, slave or free, male and female; since you are all one in Christ Jesus. And if you belong to Christ, then you are Abraham's seed, heirs according to the promise" (Gal. 3:28–29).

6. Erickson, *Christian Theology*, 498.

7. Hastings, *Encyclopedia of Religion and Ethics*, 1:122.

8. Some churches add the role of deacon to this list.

Even if you hold to a complementarian viewpoint for the current conditions on earth, the heavenly paradigm will feature an established equality among both sexes as the gender roles on earth will not carry over. For the first time in history, God will orchestrate an environment where men and women will fully understand each other because they will be one in Christ. Both misogynists and feminists may find themselves at odds with the heavenly culture. However, I suspect that we will all appreciate and endear ourselves to this newfound environment, especially as we will be perfected by this time.

## Angelic Likeness Indicates No Gender Relationships

Second, angelic likeness indicates that there is no longer any need for gender relationships as found in marriage. If genders are no longer found in heaven, then marriages are no longer necessary. This is not to say that males and females will not have common bonds and friendships. Believers in Christ will be united in a greater sense than they are now. Furthermore, this is not to say that the features of our gender will not carry over to our resurrected bodies in the sense that our bodies may look comparable to the ones currently held.[9] They potentially will, but it will no longer be found in a marital paradigm, and they will not hold the genders that are currently taken. Rather, everyone will be part of the community of Christ. Will we have individual relationships? Absolutely! But to reiterate, our relationships with the entire community of Christ will be much deeper than even the relationships we now have in marriage.

Notice that in heaven the church is called the *bride of Christ* (Rev. 21:2, 9) as we are all united to Christ and the perfected relationship that we have with him and with each other. Craig Blomberg perhaps words it best when he writes, "In the life to come, all interpersonal relationships will no doubt far surpass the most intimate and pleasurable of human intercourse as we now know it. Neither jealousy nor exclusivism will mar human interaction in any way."[10] Sexual intercourse will not be in heaven. Nonetheless, the

---

9. That is to say, we may bear a resemblance to the bodies that we now possess. Randy Alcorn takes this position a bit further than I would. He contends, "We'll never be genderless because human bodies aren't genderless. The point of the resurrection is that we will have real human bodies essentially linked to our original ones. Gender is a God-created aspect of humanity." Alcorn, *Heaven.*

10. Blomberg, *Matthew*, 333.

loving interactions that the people of God have with each other in the perfected and holy love of God in that heavenly domain will surpass the most pleasurable experiences found in sexual intercourse. If I am understanding this concept correctly, then this means that each experience of heaven will far surpass the emotional highs found in a loving marital relationship. This concept may be difficult to fathom in our sex-craved culture. Consider that human sexuality is a gift given by God to be enjoyed within the confines of marriage. If God gave a gift like sexual intercourse to be enjoyed on earth in marriage, then imagine the greater degree of love that will be found in a place than which nothing greater could be conceived.

You have probably heard the phrase "the honeymoon is over." The phrase describes a time when the individuals in a relationship begin taking each other for granted. It can also refer to a time when the employee has been with their employer so long that the thrills are now over. It is as if we anticipate a time when we will be disappointed or no longer find satisfaction in our present relationships. However, such a time won't happen in heaven. The honeymoon will never be over in heaven. Remember what was previously noted about the state of extropy in that heavenly abode. The love that we find in God and the love that we have for each other will only get better and better with each passing day. Take the fruit of the Spirit and amplify it, and you still won't be close to the experience of love that you find in heaven.

## There Are No Marriages in Heaven Because of Eternal Living (22:31–33)

Second, Jesus tells the Sadducees that marriages are not found in heaven because of the nature of eternal life. The nature and structure of marriage have received a lot of attention in recent years. What is marriage? What is the purpose of marriage? Is it a matter of love alone?

The marital construct was created not just for love, although love and companionship constitute a major element of marriage.[11] For instance, the first marital construct was found in the creation narrative in which God gave Adam a spouse[12] to have as a helpmate (Gen. 2:15–25).[13] In addition

11. Up until the past few centuries, a couple's parents arranged most marriages.

12. I.e., Eve.

13. The term ʿezer is defined as a "helper," "one who comes alongside," or "an assistant." See Swanson, Dictionary of Biblical Languages with Semitic Domains.

to love and companionship, a major theological reason behind marriage was to build a suitable and sustainable environment for children to live, learn, and mature. Worded another way, the marital construct was given so that future generations would have a safe, stable environment. Two passages of Scripture show the importance of child-rearing in the marital construct.

First, consider God's first commandment to humanity. God created both male and female in his image (Gen. 1:27) and then told them to "Be fruitful, multiply, fill the earth, and subdue it" (Gen. 1:28). Marriage is a practical concept as it was created to provide a safe environment to multiply the earth. Thomas Aquinas argues, quite correctly in my assessment, that marriage "is a sacramental union."[14] Thus, marriage was divinely gifted as a finite sacrament, or covenant, to provide a home for children.[15]

Second, the importance of parental involvement in marriage is shown in the greatest commandment. Jesus noted that the greatest commandment in Scripture was found in Deuteronomy 6:4–5 (Matt. 22:36–40). The text is known as the *Shema*, a Hebrew word meaning "hear."[16] The *Shema* states, "Listen, Israel: The LORD our God, the LORD is one. Love the LORD your God with all your heart, with all your soul, and with all your strength" (Deut. 6:4–5). It is of critical importance to place God at the first in all that we do. However, readers often stop at verse 5. After the commandment, God instructs parents to "Repeat them to your children. Talk about them when you sit in your house and when you walk along the road, when you lie down and when you get up" (Deut. 6:7). Thus, marriage provides not only a secure home, but it also gifts the parents—fathers and mothers—a safe environment to educate their children on spiritual matters. Education is an important part of the home. From the start, parents assumed the role of teachers. They did not remain absent from their children's learning.

Two things are noted regarding the uselessness of marriage relating to the eternal life experienced in heaven. In contrast to the marital construct on earth, especially considering the nature of raising future generations, eternal life does not require reproduction, and it does not require parental instruction. Let us investigate these two issues a bit more.

14. Aquinas, *Summa Theologica* LXIII.a2.o4.

15. Many law enforcement officers have told me that the absence of fathers in the home has led many young males and females to join dangerous gangs, as the gangs provide them the home that they feel they never had.

16. *Shema* is defined as "hear" or to "understand." See Strong, *Enhanced Strong's Lexicon.*

## Eternal Living Indicates No Need for Reproduction

First, as previously mentioned, marriages serve as a means to reproduce and a safe place to rear children. This is no longer necessary in heaven since Jesus said that the life to come is eternal. In one of my favorite Jesuan teachings on the matter, Jesus said, "I am the resurrection and the life. The one who believes in me, even if he dies, will live. Everyone who lives and believes in me will never die. Do you believe this?" (Jn. 11:25–26). This text is full of rich theological treasures. However, suffice it to say, Jesus assures Martha that life continues after this life and in no way ceases. As it stands, reproduction is shown to be unnecessary in heaven because of two theological points.

First, the command to multiply the earth is nullified in eternity. As previously noted, God gave the command to "be fruitful, multiply, fill the earth, and subdue it" (Gen. 1:28). Only couples that have had three or more children have fulfilled this command. Two parents must at least have two children to meet their current numerical quota. That is, there are two parents. Two children do not multiply the future generation, but it only replaces each parent. Multiplication comes when couples have three or more children.

My wife and I only have one child. It is not as if we didn't want more. Unfortunately, we suffered two miscarriages before my son was born. In addition to the miscarriages, the birth of my son was rough on my wife's body, to the point that we were unable to have more. Thus, it should be noted that not all couples can have children because of physical, financial, or emotional issues. No worries. We completely understand your pain. However, the point about multiplication is merely to note the need for larger families. Yet in heaven, this is unnecessary because the commandment to multiply no longer exists. Angels do not reproduce because they are everlasting beings.[17]

Second, in heaven, this command is nullified as people are perfected in heaven through the sanctifying work of the Holy Spirit. God will have perfected those who have gone through this life and will glorify them in eternity. The number of people in heaven appears to be set according to those who have lived through this life, at least from what we see in the pages of Scripture. Is it possible that God could create other beings in eternity? Sure, anything is possible with God. If so, that would completely be

---

17. Angels are not eternal as God is eternal. Like human beings, angels have a beginning point, but they are everlasting in their duration. God is the only being in all of reality that exists as pure actuality and pure existence.

God's prerogative. But this exceeds what can be known through the pages of Scripture. Thus, we are safer to say that it is most likely that God will not.

Before concluding this section, this brings to mind the age of accountability. What happens to people who die before they can make a profession of faith or to people who are incapable of making a profession of faith? Individuals who die before being able to recognize their sin and make a profession of faith never had the opportunity to experience the gospel message. Thus, the person cannot be said to have been consciously aware of his or her need for salvation. Therefore, I believe God allows people to enter heaven who died before reaching the age of accountability for three reasons.

First, Jesus notes that the Spirit of God convicts individuals "about sin, because they do not believe in me" (Jn. 16:9). If a person is too young to know about sin and to respond to God's grace, then such a judgment could not come. Therefore, a problem arises when trying to hold young individuals accountable who pass before reaching a mature cognitive state.

Second, the gospel is presented by hearing, understanding, and receiving. Paul notes that people are saved if we "confess with your mouth, 'Jesus is Lord,' and believe in your heart that God has raised him from the dead . . . One believes with the heart, resulting in righteousness, and one confesses with the mouth, resulting in salvation" (Rom. 10:9–10). Furthermore, Paul goes on to say, "How, then, can they call on him they have not believed in? And how can they believe without hearing about him? And how can they hear without a preacher?" (Rom. 10:14). Granted, I am non-Calvinist and believe in the Spirit's convicting power and in a person's ability to respond to the Spirit's calling. Nevertheless, Paul's teaching does seem to suggest the non-Calvinist notion as he describes the process of salvation including hearing, convicting, and receiving.[18] The process that normally occurs with a person cannot happen with a young child under normal circumstances. Therefore, one defaults to the loving grace of God, which leads us to our final point.

Third, God desires to save all (2 Pet. 3:9) and that Christ is "himself . . . the atoning sacrifice for our sins, and not only ours, but also for those of the whole world" (1 Jn. 2:2). In Ezekiel 18, God said to Israel, "Throw off all the transgressions you have committed, and get yourselves a new heart and

18. Some people say that theological matters such as these do not matter. The age of accountability is one such area that shows why these matters are incredibly important. With the Calvinist notion of election, one could never be certain whether one's young, deceased children are in heaven. Yet if one holds to God's benevolent desire to save all, then a person holds a much better reason for believing in the salvation of the innocents.

a new spirit. Why should you die, house of Israel? For I take no pleasure in anyone's death.' This is the declaration of the Lord God. 'So repent and live!' (Ezek. 18:31–32). I truly worry about preachers who preach on hell as if they desire to send people there. It is almost as if some take sadistic pleasure in speaking about the condemnation of others. Such actions do not reflect the heart of God, as God truly desires to save all people. If God has such a heart to save, then why would he condemn young innocents who could not respond to God's Spirit or repent from their sins? In my opinion, I believe that children who die young are escorted into the loving hands of Jesus himself. Taking all of this under consideration, I think we can accept the notion of the age of accountability.[19]

## Eternal Living Indicates No Need for Parenting

Forgive me if there is a bit of repetition here, but it is necessary to emphasize the distinction between the way things exist now and the way they will be. While marriages serve as a means to parent the next generation, this is no longer necessary in heaven. First, in heaven, everyone is going to be perfected. We will be made in the likeness of Christ and, therefore, will no longer need parental guidance. Since there is no sin in heaven, then no parental pep talks are necessary. That is not to say that education ends in heaven. I believe that we will continue to learn for all eternity. However, parents no longer need to warn sons and daughters about the ills of life, because there will be no ills of life in heaven.

Second, God will serve as our perfect Parent. As we have discussed previously, God will be our God and we will be his people. He will serve as the ultimate parent to all of us. Quite honestly, he already is.

The Lord's Prayer reveals just how powerful God's parental traits are. Notice Jesus begins by saying, "Our Father in heaven, your name be honored as holy" (Matt. 6:9). Here Jesus addresses God as *abba*. The term was not used until after Jesus's ministry that Jewish rabbis use the term in their prayers. Craig Blomberg writes, "Use of this intimate term for God (almost equivalent to the English "Daddy") was virtually unparalleled in

---

19. In Jewish thought, people were not accountable until the age of 12 or 13. However, certain youth may prove accountable enough prior to this age to make a conscientious decision to follow Christ. I was around the age of 7 when I followed Christ. The age of accountability depends on each person's developmental growth and spiritual maturity.

first-century Judaism."[20] For Jesus, God was not a distant, uncaring, deadbeat dad. Rather, God was intimately involved with creation and especially his people.

Throughout the NT, God is portrayed similarly. Paul notes that believers are God's children because "God sent the Spirit of his Son into our hearts, crying, '*Abba,* Father!' So you are no longer a slave but a son, and if a son, then God has made you an heir" (Gal. 4:6–7). In Hebrews 12:6, the writer of Hebrews references Proverbs 3:12 to show how God disciplines and corrects his children to shape them into the people they need to be.[21]

The discipline of the Lord is not something that we may necessarily enjoy. I recall a moment from my childhood when I received my report card which held some pretty bad grades in math. My dad had warned me that I needed to better memorize the multiplication table. As much as it pained me to admit it, he was right. The bus ride home was especially long that afternoon, as I knew that I had to face the music. My dad did not whip me for bad marks, but he did manage to give some lengthy and eloquent lectures on the importance of having a hard work ethic. Some may have argued that a whipping may have been the better option. Nonetheless, I know that my dad elucidated his lengthy life lessons out of his love for me and my good.

When we get to heaven, we are still going to help one another in heaven and will continue to need God's parental love. But, since we are all perfected, we no longer need human parental guidance. Since there is no sin, there is no need for parental warnings or admonitions. Thus, the human parental office is no longer necessary.

## There Are No Marriages in Heaven Because of Everlasting Love (22:34–40)

Third, and finally, marriages will not exist in heaven because of the everlasting love we all experience. Individuals who have expressed concern about marriages not existing in heaven classically note three reasons why they wished their marriages would continue in heaven—1) companionship, 2) love, and 3) sexuality. Sex is desirable due to the emotional and hormonal connectedness we experience with our beloved ones. The pleasure of sexual

20. Blomberg, *Matthew,* 119.

21. "For the Lord disciplines the one he loves, just as a father disciplines the son in whom he delights" (Prov. 3:12).

encounters is replaced with perfect spiritual joy. But the desired traits of companionship and love are multiplied in the higher form of love found in heaven. The everlasting love of heaven is characterized by two expressions.

## Everlasting Love Comes from Our God's Love

First, while marital love is great, it pales in comparison to the love that God holds for us. This divine love surpasses any physical experience of love that could be mustered from our earthly affairs. Consider that human love would not be possible if it were not first for the love that God expressed for us. The apostle John reminds us that "We love because [God] first loved us" (1 Jn. 4:19). Thus, love itself is only possible because God first initiated and granted the world with the gift of love. Part of the Anselmian understanding of God is rooted in the belief that God is the greatest good. Anselm prayerfully deduces that "So truly, therefore, dost thou exist, O Lord, my God, that thou canst not be conceived not to exist; and rightly. For, if a mind could conceive of a being better than thee, the creature would rise above the Creator; and this is most absurd."[22] If God is the ultimate good, then he is omnibenevolent.[23]

How has God expressed his love for humanity thus far? First, notice Jesus's connection of Abraham and Isaac with the ever-living, ever-present God. Even though these men died ages ago, Jesus says that they are still alive because God "is not a God of the dead, but of the living" (22:32). Thus, these individuals continue to exist in the gracious watch-care of God because of God's loving nature. Heaven itself is only possible because of God's great love.

Second, our existence and being both serve as evidence of God's love. As Adam Harwood notes, "The act of creating people was an act of love."[24] Not only is our creation an act of divine love, but so is our continued reality. Anthony Thiselton argues that "Our existence and birth in the first place, and then every breath that we take, are equally gifts of God's love."[25] Thus, marital love is only possible because of the creative loving nature of God. Love in any sense is a direct result of the love that first emanates from God's

22. Anselm, *Proslogium* 3, in Anselm, *Proslogium; Monologium*, 9.

23. That is, all-loving.

24. Harwood, *Christian Theology*, 182.

25. Thiselton, *Systematic Theology*, 46.

divine love. Remember that Aquinas reminds us that God is the only being in all of space and time that exists as pure act.[26]

If God is love (1 Jn. 4:16) and exists as pure act, then it stands to reason that love itself is only possible because of God's existence. And, if God is the source of love, then the love that believers feel from God for them in heaven exceeds any kind of love experienced on earth. In our spiritual state in heaven after death, we will experience the richness of God's love. Thomas Oden said, "Scripture portrays believers as engaged in a conscious life in dialogue, in communion with God immediately after death (2 Cor. 5:8; Phil. 1:23; Rev. 6:9; 20:4)."[27] The believer's state in heaven can be likened to a spiritual rest. Martin Luther said that this state of existence is like a "deep strong, sweet sleep' considering the 'coffin as nothing other than our Lord Jesus' bosom or *Paradise,* the grave as nothing other than a soft couch or ease of rest' (Luther, *Christian Songs, Latin and German, for Use at Funerals, WML* 6:287)."[28] Therefore, in our resurrection state after Christ's return, we will experience even more of the depth and richness of God's love.

A robust understanding of the divine love expressed in heaven holds a transformative impact on the earthly life of the believer. Athanasius of Alexandria noted that early Christians did not fear death as much when they realized the reality of the resurrection. He noted that in Alexandria, where persecution was harsh during the Diocletian persecution of AD 303–5, many courageous Christian women would laugh at the fires of their persecution because, as Athanasius put it, they "despise even what is naturally fearful."[29]

Unfortunately, our relationships on earth are often broken. Some of you may have faced divorce due to irreconcilable issues confronted in the marital relationship. Others may have never married. Perhaps you have lived under the illusion that you would find Mr. or Mrs. Right, but that person never arrived. Still yet, others may be in difficult relationships that

26. "First, because it was shown above that there is some first being, whom we call God; and that this first being must be pure act, without the admixture of any potentiality, for the reason that, absolutely, potentiality is posterior to act. Now everything which is in any way changed, is in some way in potentiality. Hence it is evident that it is impossible for God to be in any way changeable." Aquinas, *Summa Theologica* 1q.3a.2, in *A Summa of the Summa,* 105.

27. Oden, *Classic Christianity,* 786.

28. Oden, *Classic Christianity,* 786.

29. Athanasius, *Incarnation of the Word* 27, 44, in Oden, *Classical Christianity,* 790–91.

never seem to reach the point of holy matrimony. Others may have wonderful relationships filled with great times and wonderful adventures. Some of you may be in a long-term marriage but feel alone, without any sense of passion, to the point that you and your partner feel more like roommates than lovers. No matter which category you fit in, your relationship with God in heaven will be far richer, far more intense, and far deeper than any relationship you may have encountered on earth. But our relationship with God is not the only experience of love that we will have in heaven. There is yet another dimension of love in that celestial abode.

## Everlasting Love Comes from Our Christian Love

Second, marital relationships are not needed in heaven because of the love that we will have for one another. The NT often calls the church the bride of Christ (Matt. 25:1–13; Jn. 3:29; Eph. 5:25–27; 2 Cor. 11:2; and Rev. 19:7–9; 21:2, 9). The NT uses the singular term for bride and not brides. Thus, the people of God are interconnected in a covenant relationship with God. In many ways, believers are like the roots of a forest that are interconnected. If one tree is affected, then other trees are impacted because of their shared system.

The interconnectedness of believers is viewed by the ecological theology portrayed in Scripture. The Greek term *oikos* refers to the earth or a dwelling place. Paul uses the term in Romans 16:5 when he discusses the body of the church. Paul writes, "Greet also the church that meets in their home (*oikos*)" (Rom. 16:5). The growth of the church is likened to an organism growing in creation. In like manner, Jesus likens heaven to an ecological relationship. Using the same term *oikos*, Jesus states, "In my Father's house (*oikos*) are many rooms. If it were not so, would I have told you that I am going to prepare a place for you?" (Jn. 14:2). Thus, the people of God are interconnected in a fashion far deeper than what is realized.

Being interconnected in this fashion, the people of God will be able to love one another as Christ loves us. Just as our love for God will be perfected, so our love for one another will be perfected. People are often hurt in church, some to the point that they do not desire to attend church any longer. Those issues will be non-existent in heaven. We will finally be able to love one another as Christ envisioned when he instituted the church.

## Conclusion

Someone once asked Billy Graham, "How did you get such a high status? No offense, but I have heard preachers who are more eloquent than you. How in the world did you get to where you are?" Graham humbly responded, "If you see a turtle on a fence post, do you ask how the turtle climbed the post, or do you not suppose that someone placed the turtle on the fencepost? I am that turtle that God placed on a fence post." When someone else asked him the same question, he also said, "I plan to ask God that very thing."

Marriages are wonderful and important institutions that God created for us. They are institutions of love designed to bring forth the next generation. However, marriages will not extend into heaven because of our newfound likeness in heaven. While our marriages are important, and we should emphasize them greatly, they are not meant to carry over to heaven. (Some may celebrate, while others may mourn this fact.) We will be like angels in heaven, though we will not be angels. Marriages will not carry over into heaven because of our new life. We will be perfected in heaven. We do not need to reproduce and will not need human parenting because God is our Parent. Marriages will not carry over into heaven because of our love. Our love for God will be perfected as will our love for each other.

Like many people, Sandy was a bit taken aback by the notion that marriages will not extend into heaven. However, when we discussed the great depth of love and companionship found in our heavenly home, she found a great deal of peace with the concept. Like Sandy, many people struggle with the notion that marriages cease at death, especially those with stellar marriages. But this should come as no surprise because our marriage vows always end with the words "till death do us part." Healthy, loving marriages serve as a metaphor for the loving relationship we fully experience with God and the church in our heavenly home. Instead of dread, this should provide a great sense of joy. Besides, if both parties of marriage have a covenant relationship with Christ, then they will be bound by these heavenly interconnections. As such, each member of the marriage will experience an even greater love for one another in heaven than what was thought possible in this current sphere of existence.

# Chapter Eight

# ARE NEAR-DEATH EXPERIENCES REAL?

## 2 Corinthians 12:1–10

M Y CONVERSATION WITH SANDY took an unexpected twist. Sandy asked, "I have heard some people say that when we die, we just die. We do not live on until Christ returns. Why isn't it that we just simply die when we die? Why do we need to live on in eternity?" Honestly, I was stunned by this question. For me, the knowledge that life continues into eternity brings me great hope. For Sandy, however, she implied that simply passing into nothingness was comforting, much akin to being eternally under anesthesia.

Our conversation traveled in a different direction at this juncture. I noted the biblical evidence supporting the continuation of the soul. However, we also began discussing the often misunderstood and controversial notion of near-death experiences (NDEs). NDEs are real experiences that explicitly deny naturalism and implicitly abduce the existence of the afterlife.

One popular story speaks of three knuckleheads who died in a car accident and appeared before the pearly gates. Saint Peter addressed the first one, "Before you are allowed to enter heaven you must answer this question. What can you tell me about Easter?" The first knucklehead looked puzzled for a moment then said, "Oh, I know. That's the holiday in the Fall when you stuff your face with turkey and watch football games all day." "Wrong!" replied Peter as the first knucklehead disappeared in a puff of smoke. Peter then turned to the second knucklehead and asked him, "What can *you* tell me about Easter?" "Isn't that the holiday in December when you buy gifts for people and decorate a dead tree?" "Wrong!" replied Peter as the second knucklehead disappeared in a puff of smoke. Peter then turned to the third knucklehead who was trembling with fear. Peter asked him, "What can *you* tell me about Easter?" The last knucklehead replied, "Well that is the holiday that occurs in early spring. It begins on the day Jesus was hung on a cross between two criminals and was made to wear a crown of thorns. He died and they buried him in a cave. Then they rolled a big rock over the cave's entrance to seal it. Then on the third day, the cave was opened, and Jesus rose from the dead. So, every year, if Jesus pops his head out of the grave that year it means six more weeks of winter." Saint Peter shook his head in disbelief.

NDEs are just as misunderstood as the third knucklehead's understanding of Easter. Do some stories presented in NDE books grant information that should be held with a grain of salt? Of course! However, some pastors and theologians have thrown out all possibilities of NDEs due to some of the more suspicious stories. This is most unfortunate. Theologically and logically, such extreme takes are irresponsible.

NDE stands for *near-death experiences*. French psychologist and epistemologist Victor Egger first coined the term in the 1890s as an "experience de mort imminente" (experience of imminent death). NDE researcher Raymond Moody later popularized the term near-death experiences as we now use it. We will describe and define NDEs and their counterpart OBEs. Then, we will examine the evidence for NDEs/OBEs, provide objective evidence for NDEs, and grant biblical support for NDEs, before concluding with the impact that NDEs hold on religion and philosophy. I am excited to take this journey with you.

## Explaining NDEs and OBEs

Before we move on, we need to first explain what we mean by NDEs and note their characteristics of NDEs. As previously noted, NDEs stand for *near-death experiences*. A near-death experience occurs when a person dies and has conscious experiences outside and beyond the body. These experiences may include observations of the room, building, and location in which the person's body is found. The experience often includes seeing a bright light, feelings of peace and serenity, meeting God and religious figures, and being greeted by deceased family members. People often report having extra-sensory abilities that are currently unavailable (i.e., seeing colors that are not found on earth, and the experience of timelessness, among other abilities). To be classified as an NDE, these conscious occurrences happen after the person is declared dead.

While the focus of our chapter will be on NDEs, it is important to speak on OBEs which stand for *out-of-body experiences*. OBEs are like NDEs in the fact that the person experiences conscious experiences outside of the physical body. However, OBEs may not always accompany death encounters. Some have reported experiencing OBEs during meditative practices and drug-induced states.

The main differentiation between NDEs and OBEs is that the person is declared dead during an NDE, whereas OBEs occur while the body still has life. The popular story of 4-year-old Colton Burpo's trip to heaven, as found in the popular book *Heaven is for Real,* is an example of an OBE because Colton was not officially dead when the event occurred. His heavenly experience happened while he was on an operating table.

OBEs are extremely interesting and hold significant value. However, the objective impact of NDEs far outweighs OBEs. This is not to say that some OBEs cannot hold value in demonstrating the existence of an afterlife and substance dualism. However, the absence of brainwaves in NDE experiences affords an added layer of evidential proof against claims of hallucinations that OBEs cannot provide. Additionally, reports of OBEs tend to provide more anecdotal data than objective evidence. For that reason, our investigation will focus on NDEs rather than OBEs.

# Evidence for NDEs

One of the most consistent objections to NDEs is that the accounts offer more anecdotal subjectives rather than objective facts. Paul Kurtz, writing against the work of Raymond Moody, says, "There is no reliable evidence that people who report such experiences have died and returned, or that consciousness exists separate from the brain or body."[1] Is Kurtz right in his assessment? If so, our whole time together is for naught. Thankfully, NDEs stand on solid footing. Let us consider some lines of objective evidence supporting NDEs after first explaining the preference for objective evidence over subjective varieties.

## Preference for Objective Evidence over Subjective Evidence

Before considering the evidence, we should take a moment to describe the difference between objective and subjective evidence. Objective evidence can be confirmed outside of personal experience, whereas subjective evidence can only be found in the trustworthiness of an individual's testimony. For instance, if a person claims to have almost run into a fallen oak tree on the road on which he or she was traveling, their claim can be confirmed by external factors. Others could see the wood, leaves, and debris from the fallen tree. Perhaps one would find the trunk which formerly held the tree in place. Broken ground and objects destroyed by the tree could serve as evidence of the person's near encounter with the tree. Likewise, NDEs can be confirmed by external evidence observed by the conscious disembodied observer which can be corroborated by conscious embodied observers. So, for instance, if Person A claims to have died and seen a pencil lying on top of a cabinet in their disembodied state, Person B can check to corroborate or deny Person A's claim. This provides some strength. But if Person A claims to have seen a pencil on top of a cabinet, heard the conversation that a family member had in another room, and described seeing a deceased loved one whom Person A had never met, then, the case for Person A's NDE increases.[2]

---

1. Kurtz, *Toward a New Enlightenment*, 349.

2. While objective evidence is preferred, subjective evidence can hold some value. Subjective evidence is found only in the person describing the event in question. As such, the event cannot be independently evaluated except by the person's own testimony. Subjective experiences can be evaluated to some degree by corroborating the person's report of seeing a person that they claimed to have never known. In other cases, the collected

## Objective Evidence for NDEs

NDEs can be accepted as authentic events by five lines of objective evidence provided by numerous case studies. Others could have been added, but these provide a good foundation for the task ahead.

### *Verifying objects outside of the body*

Numerous people who have had NDE events describe seeing objects outside their bodies. In some cases, they observe objects which could have never been seen from their perspective while lying on a gurney or operating table. For instance, Kimberly Clark Sharp tells the story of a lady named Maria who experienced an NDE during her first visit to Seattle, Washington. While at Harborview Hospital in Seattle, Maria told Sharpe that she had an NDE in which she viewed a blue tennis shoe on the ledge of the hospital's roof around the corner where she had first entered the facility. It was impossible to view the shoe from the ground. Maria described a worn place on the toe of the shoe and lace found under the heel.[3] Sharp later confirmed the shoe was in the exact location where Maria had reported.

### *Verifying events outside of the body*

Events that could have never otherwise been known are reported by some who experience NDEs. NDEs can often become humorous. Such was the case with a young lady who was in the hospital and nearing death. She left her body and visited her relatives in the waiting room which was several rooms down from her own. While viewing her relatives in a disembodied state, she overheard her brother-in-law state that he was going to wait around to see if she "kicked the bucket." After she returned to her body and recovered, she confronted her brother-in-law and asked him why he wanted to wait to see if she would "kick the bucket," which understandably left her brother-in-law utterly shocked and overwhelmed.[4]

transformation of the experiences of numerous individuals can be analyzed. Thus, while objective evidence surpasses its subjective counterpart in evidential matters, that is not to say that subjective experiences never hold some warrant.

3. Habermas and Moreland, *Beyond Death*, 212.

4. This report is verified by Katie, the lady who had the NDE, and her pediatrician who revived her. Morse and Perry, *Closer to the Light*, 3–9. See also Habermas and Moreland, *Beyond Death*, 158; Moody, Lecture, Lousiana State University.

## Verifying places outside of the body

One report describes the events surrounding an NDE of an 11-year-old boy who suffered a cardiac arrest while in the hospital. He had no heartbeat for at least 20 minutes. During his 20 minutes without a heartbeat, the young boy described himself as watching the events of the emergency room from the ceiling. After his recovery, he was able to accurately convey the medical procedures the doctors and nurses performed, the colors of the instruments in the ER and where they could be found, genders of the medical personnel, and even recounted their discussions.[5] All of the boy's reports were confirmed by the medical staff.

## Vision in people who were physically blind

Several instances of NDEs have been documented by those who were physically blind but reported visual experiences while outside the body post-death. Habermas and Moreland describe one such instance in the following report.

> A chemist, for example, after being blinded a year earlier in an accident, correctly reported the visual details surrounding his near-death experience. Other individuals who had been blind for years (and were even tested for blindness again afterward) accurately described the design and colors of clothing and jewelry worn by those around them when they almost died.[6]

Interestingly, those who were physically blind and accurately reported visual experiences outside the body lost their vision when returning to the body. There is simply no physical way to account for their accurate postmortem visual experiences.

In a 2008 study, Kenneth Ring interviewed 21 blind people who described confirmed visual experiences during their NDE events, 14 of whom were blind from birth.[7] Ring's peer-reviewed study supported four conclusions: 1) NDEs are the same for individuals who are blind or visually impaired as they are for those who can physically see; 2) blind and visually impaired persons describe the same kind of visual perceptions as the

5. Habermas and Moreland, *Beyond Death,* 119; Morse and Perry, *Closer to the Light,* 24–26, 165.

6. Habermas and Moreland, *Beyond Death,* 158.

7. Ring and Cooper, *Mindsight,* 136.

visually unimpaired; 3) some of these reports can be validated by outside witnesses; 4) preliminary evidence corroborates that visual experiences do occur in NDEs.[8] These reports may potentially serve as a slam-dunk piece of evidence in favor of post-mortem soul survival.

### Conscious experiences while brain dead (Eben Alexander)

Eben Alexander is a medical doctor who served as an academic neurosurgeon for over 25 years. Alexander was left in a coma due to his diagnosis of bacterial meningitis. Most interestingly, while he experienced the events of his NDE/OBE, only the most primitive parts of his brain, termed the "housekeeping parts," were operating. The portions of the brain that store memories, observe, and are associated with hallucinations were all gone and non-functioning.[9] For all intent and purposes, Alexander's NDE discounts any proposed theory associating NDEs with hallucinations in all cases.

## Biblical Evidence for NDEs

Interestingly, some of the biggest pushback against NDEs often comes from the Christian community. Even well-renown preachers such as Dr. Robert Jeffress, pastor of the FBC Dallas, doubt the validity of NDEs because of misinterpretations of biblical texts and misunderstandings of NDEs themselves. However, we can show three passages of Scripture that seemingly authenticate the possibility of NDEs.

### Paul's Visit to the Third Heaven

First, as was noted previously, it may shock individuals to consider that the apostle Paul records his account of an NDE. In 2 Corinthians 12:1–10, Paul discusses his NDE by speaking of himself in the third person. Notice that he mentions that he was taken to the third heaven, indicating that he left the earth, the universe, and was taken into God's abode. Paul's experience of heaven left him puzzled and amazed. He realizes that he may have been out of the body. Yet he heard words that he could only describe as "inexpressible" (2 Cor. 12:4). It is also in 2 Corinthians where Paul reflects on

8. Burke, *Imagine Heaven*, 36–37.

9. Alexander, *Proof of Heaven*, 135.

his desire to be "absent from the body and at home with the Lord" (2 Cor. 5:8), possibly hinting back to the amazing heavenly encounter discussed in 2 Corinthians 12.

## John's Out-of-Body Experiences in Revelation

Second, on at least three occasions, John records being carried away by God "in the Spirit" (Revelation 4:2; 17:3; and 21:10). These encounters almost always include visual and audible experiences, many of which could not be described except through the use of allegorical symbols (e.g., horns, eyes, numbers, and so on). While the case of John is not as strong as Paul's, one can still adduce that John experienced some kind of a surreal out-of-body experience as the contents of Revelation was being communicated to him.

## Jesus's Promise to Thief on the Cross

The third and final text does not serve as a proof text indicating one's personal NDE, but rather it is a promise which describes the spiritual life that continues after death. While handing on the cross, one of the criminals begs forgiveness and asks Jesus to remember him when he enters his heavenly kingdom. Jesus responds by saying, "Truly I tell you, today you will be with me in paradise" (Luke 23:43). Jesus promises the thief that he would consciously enter the heavenly kingdom immediately following his death. To deny a continued spiritual existence as illustrated by NDEs would make Jesus a liar.

## Impact on Religion and Philosophy

To conclude, NDEs impact the nature of religion and philosophy in five powerful ways. NDEs serve as evidence of God's existence, an afterlife, and the immaterial soul. NDEs serve as a defeater of materialism and verify the soul survival viewpoint of the intermediate state. Each section will be briefly discussed below. While some of the material may be philosophically deep for the layperson, it is still worthy of the reader's time and attention.

## Serves as Evidence for God

First, if NDEs are true, then the numerous encounters that people have with God further serve as evidence for his existence. For many, their NDEs drew them closer to God and caused some who were previously skeptics to begin a life of religious devotion. Some NDE deniers claim that NDEs are the work of the devil. If so, the devil is an extremely poor tactician since people almost always draw closer to God after their encounters. Thousands of individuals from across the world have had an NDE encounter. Of them, nearly 65 percent describe experiencing a light that they associated with God. These individuals are from across the world and from various faith traditions.[10] Yet they all experience similar things when it comes to God's presence—such as feelings of peace, inexpressible love, and the most brilliant light that one has ever seen, even though the light did not harm their eyes.

## Serves as Evidence for the Afterlife

Second, if NDEs are true, then they provide evidence that life continues after death. Heavenly encounters provide just a foretaste of the glorious beauty that awaits a person after their passing. Even though death still brings anxiety to an individual as it is a completely new experience, the fear involved with death quickly loses steam when considering the numerous reports of serenity and love felt in that heavenly dwelling. Many, if not the vast majority, of those who have had an NDE report that they no longer fear death after returning. Some have argued that these experiences are just chemical-induced experiences flowing from a dying brain. However, the skeptic has difficulty explaining how individuals report objects and conversations held outside the body that a person could not have otherwise known. Additionally, the skeptic cannot account for cases where a person encounters family members who had previously deceased and were otherwise unknown to the person meeting them.

10. See the Near-Death Experience Research Foundation (https://nderf.org) to read firsthand some of these encounters. At the time of publication, the site has recorded over 5,000 cases worldwide.

## Serves as Evidence for the Conscious Immaterial Soul

Third, if NDEs are true, then they serve as additional proof for the existence of a person's conscious immaterial soul. A person cannot be said to be exclusively a body, but rather he or she has a part of their being that transcends the physical world. This is to be expected since God is Spirit (John 4:24) and made us into his image (Gen. 1:27). Two philosophical perspectives concerning the human state are important to dissect as we move on with our study. Philosophers are generally divided into two camps: monists and dualists. Monists argue that human beings consist of a singular physical makeup. Typically, monists deny that consciousness or a human soul exists separately from the physical body. They also contend that the brain produces consciousness through chemical reactions and the like, giving the impression that a person is a conscious soul. Theologian Stanley Grenz is an example of a Christian who holds to a mildly monistic interpretation.[11]

In contrast, dualists contend that a person consists of a body and a soul. While the two intersect, they are two different substances. Dualists often argue that the body and soul are meant to exist together, but that death brings a temporary separation of the two. J. P. Moreland of Biola University is a strong proponent of Cartesian dualism, also known as substance dualism. Thomas Aquinas argued for a form of dualism known as *hylomorphism*.[12] He held that the immaterial soul served as the basis from which the body is made. A lot more could be added to this conversation. Nonetheless, hylomorphism is a philosophically rich form of dualism as Aquinas blends the Platonism of Augustine of Hippo with the metaphysics of Aristotle. While we will not assert which of the two forms of dualism is correct, we only mention these two forms of dualism to note the depth that is found in the concept.

If NDEs are true, then dualism is most assuredly proven correct and monism is falsified. How the immaterial soul blends and interacts with the physical world is another topic of discussion that expands beyond the scope of our discussion. Nonetheless, NDEs hold both theological and

---

11. While Grenz is open to some form of an intermediate state, he seemingly presents the state of existence merely as one that awaits the resurrection without full consciousness. Grenz denies the concept that one is automatically transported to the resurrection, but his viewpoint comes close to the ideology. Grenz, *Theology for the Community of God,* 597.

12. Hylomorphism combines two Greek words: *hyle* meaning "matter," and *morphe* meaning "form" or "appearance."

philosophical ramifications, which may explain why some are so adamantly opposed to such experiences.

## Serves as a Defeater of Materialism

Fourth, the present deduction follows from the third. As noted, NDEs hold philosophical ramifications. If NDEs are true and human beings possess a conscious immaterial soul, then materialism—the idea that the material world is all that exists—is most assuredly falsified. Materialism cannot account for the verifiable and testable encounters that NDEs afford.

## Provides Evidence for Soul Survival

Fifth, while many others could be mentioned, we will discuss five major views on what happens to the soul after death. Some of these viewpoints were covered earlier in the book. Nevertheless, it is important to revisit these concepts as we show the impact of NDEs. As you will see, NDEs defend the classic orthodox notion of soul survival.

### *Soul Death—Monism*

The first view is called *soul death*. Advocates of this view contend that the soul dies with the body. Thus, there is no life beyond the scope of the natural body. In naturalistic circles, this is a common belief. The belief has surprisingly gained traction in some Christian circles where it is sometimes called *Christian mortalism*. It may come as a surprise that some Protestant Reformers, even possibly Martin Luther, held to this view. One of the earliest mentions of Christian mortalism came from Eusebius of Caesarea who wrote that a group in Arabia was proclaiming that the soul ceased to exist at death. Origen traveled to speak to them and persuaded them to cast aside this foreign doctrine. Eusebius writes,

> About the same time others arose in Arabia, putting forward a doctrine foreign to the truth. They said that during the present time the human soul dies and perishes with the body, but that at the time of the resurrection they will be renewed together. And at that time also a synod of considerable size assembled, and Origen, being again

invited thither, spoke publicly on the question with such effect that the opinions of those who had formerly fallen were changed.[13]

Origen's identification of the soul death theory with a "doctrine foreign to the truth"[14] illustrates well that soul survival is not a new Christian doctrine but finds itself rooted in the early church. Rather, the monistic viewpoint is the new kid on the block.

### Soul Sleep—Monism—The Soul Ceases to Exist at Death

*Soul sleep* is comparable to soul death. The only difference is that the soul is believed to sleep during the time of the intermediate state. Some view the concept of soul sleep almost in the likes of a time warp, where one is automatically transported to the resurrection even though thousands of years may have passed. The *Amazing Facts* ministries which are associated with the Seventh Day Adventist Church gravitate toward either soul sleep or soul death. Since NDEs are verifiable according to objective evidence, the theory of soul sleep is found far less probable.

### Transmigrational Oneness—The Soul is Reincarnated in Other Lives

In New Age philosophies, eastern religious concepts are incorporated into viewpoints on the intermediate state. Some claim that the soul continues to reincarnate until the person finds oneness with God. NDEs cannot deny the possibility that transmigrational oneness occurs. However, they do not tend to advocate for the position either. For those who meet people who have previously died in their NDE encounters, transmigrational oneness would appear to be false. From a Christian perspective, reincarnation does not find a clear defense, especially in light of the formidable teachings on the resurrection.[15] If reincarnation is true and the resurrection is true, then which of a person's lives are resurrected? This leads to absurdity. When considering the evidence for the resurrection of Christ, then soul survival leading to resurrection makes more sense of NDEs than transmigrational oneness.

13. Eusebius of Caesarea, *Church History* 6.37.1, 279.

14. Eusebius of Caesarea, *Church History* 6.37.1, 279.

15. Some have argued that at least some in early Judaism believed in reincarnation, as some groups were looking for the return of Elijah in a new body (Matt. 17:12–13). Even Herod seemed to suggest that Jesus was the reincarnated John the Baptist (Matt. 14:1–2).

## Gnosticism—Disembodied Soul Lives on Forever with No Resurrection

Gnosticism was one of the earliest heresies denounced by the church. Gnostics claim that the spiritual world is good and that the material world is evil. As such, the soul lives outside of the body, never to return. Thus, ideas of the resurrection are foreign to Gnostic concepts. NDEs do not necessarily differentiate between Gnosticism and the resurrection concepts found within the traditional soul survival model. Gnosticism is denounced by the historical resurrection of Jesus of Nazareth and the Christian teachings of a new heaven and a new earth.

## Soul Survival/Soul Continuationism—The Soul Lives in a Conscious, Spiritual State Until the Resurrection

Soul survival most closely aligns with the Christian perspective. In the soul survival model, the soul continues to exist outside of the body during the intermediate state. At the resurrection, the soul is reunited with the body in a new spiritual-material-perfected form. Several passages of Scripture defend the concept of soul survival. Let's examine four of them.

### LUKE 23:43: WORDS OF JESUS ON THE CROSS

While hanging on the cross, one of the criminals begs forgiveness and asks Jesus to remember him when he enters his heavenly kingdom. Jesus responds by saying, "Truly I tell you, today you will be with me in paradise" (Luke 23:43). Jesus promises the thief that he would consciously enter the heavenly kingdom immediately following his death. He did not say, "Tomorrow, you will be with me in paradise," "At the final resurrection, you will be with me in paradise," or "You will fall asleep, and time warp to the final resurrection where you will be with me in paradise." No! Jesus's statement presented a state of immediacy. To deny a continued spiritual existence as illustrated by NDEs would make Jesus a liar.

### LUKE 16:19–31: PARABLE OF THE RICH MAN AND LAZARUS

In the Parable of the Rich Man and Lazarus, Jesus tells the story of two men who died—one who was a poor man of faith named Lazarus, and the other one was an unnamed rich man. Lazarus went to Paradise, whereas the rich man went to Hades. It is important to note that the two men went to these spiritual abodes immediately after their deaths. Additionally, the rich man asked Father Abraham to warn his brothers, who were still living, to repent and avoid coming to Hades. Abraham said that they had Moses and the Prophets, a summarization that described the totality of the Word of God. The rich man said that if a person were to rise from the dead, then they might believe. Abraham replied that if they did not believe the Word of God, then they would not believe even if a man were to rise from the dead. Concerning our topic today, the brothers were still alive while the rich man and Lazarus had died. Yet, they were still conscious and alive in a spiritual state.

## JOHN 11:25–26: "I AM THE RESURRECTION AND THE LIFE"

In John 11:25–26, Jesus tells Martha that the one who lives and believes in him will never die. In the Greek language, Jesus said (literally translated) "and everyone who lives and believes in me will no, not, never die, forever." The triple negative serves as an intensifier which indicates absolute certitude. Thus, it is an impossibility for the one who lives in Christ to ever truly die.

## 2 CORINTHIANS 12:1–10: PAUL'S NDE

As previously noted, Paul records his account of an NDE. In 2 Corinthians 12:1–10, Paul discusses his NDE by speaking of himself in the third person. Notice that he mentions that he was taken to the third heaven, indicating that he left the earth, the universe, and was taken into God's abode. Paul's experience of heaven left him puzzled and amazed. He realizes that he may have been out of the body. Yet he heard words that he could only describe as "inexpressible" (2 Cor. 12:4). It is also in 2 Corinthians where Paul reflects on his desire to be "absent from the body and at home with the Lord" (2 Cor. 5:8), possibly hinting back to the amazing heavenly encounter discussed in 2 Corinthians 12.

## Common Objections Against NDEs

Oddly, some of the most common objections against NDEs do not come from skeptics but from believers. The final section of this chapter will look at common objections given against NDEs and how we can respond to them. The following objections are normally conveyed: NDEs are the work of the devil and/or the New Age; NDEs are hallucinations; NDEs provide a false sense of hope; NDEs are unbiblical; and NDEers give conflicting information about their experiences.

## NDEs are Works of the Devil/New Age

Dr. Robert Jeffress, the pastor of FBC Dallas, wrote concerning NDEs,

> Many accounts of near-death experiences are similar to the occult. For example, both the occult and near-death experiences involve out-of-body experiences and contact with those on the other side. And in both the occult and near-death experiences, people claim to have psychic powers. Some claim the power of clairvoyance–the ability to discern information about the past, present, or future by unnatural means. Some claim to have telepathy–the ability to send or receive messages by people's thoughts. If they have that power, then that power did not come from the kingdom of light. It came from the kingdom of darkness. Any claims of psychic powers are associated with Satan himself.[16]

Jeffress appears to hold that God and angels cannot appear as light-bearing beings. He undergirds his argument by holding that Satan disguises himself as an angel of light. But wait! Why would Satan disguise himself as an angel of light if God and angels were not light-bearing beings?

Furthermore, the Bible depicts God and angels as beings of light. For instance, 1 John 1:5 says, "God is light, and there is absolutely no darkness in him" (1 John 1:5). In the book of Revelation, Jesus is shrouded with a dazzling appearance of light. In addition to having brilliant hair of white and bronzed skin, John writes that Jesus's "face was shining like the sun at full strength" (Rev. 1:16). Throughout Scripture, divine theophanies are almost always accompanied by incomprehensibly brilliant light (see also Eze. 1:27; 8:2; Psa. 94:1; 50:2; Eze.43:2; Hos. 6:5; and Eze. 10:4). Even God's angels appear in a brilliant display of light. When the angel stood before

16. Jeffress, "Principles to Evaluate Near-Death Experiences," para. 3.

Mary, the "glory of the Lord shone around them; and they were terribly frightened" (Luke 2:9).

Paul teaches that Satan often masquerades himself as an angel of light. However, the text does not teach what Jeffress implies. Paul writes, "For Satan disguises himself as an angel of light" (2 Cor. 11:13). At face value, it may seem like Jeffress's comments are valid; that is, until one evaluates the context of the passage of Scripture. Paul speaks to individuals of the church who allow Satan to persuade them to focus on more material things—such as their preferred preacher or preferred charity—than to focus on the spiritual mission of God. Satan, in this case, imitates God's good plan, leading to the common phrase, "the road to hell is paved with good intentions."

## NDEs are Hallucinations

Due to the nature of many NDEs, hallucinations are no longer viable explanations. People have reported seeing events, people, and objects that could have never been otherwise known except for an out-of-body experience. Of all the objections, the hallucination theory is the most prominent. But it is becoming easier to dismiss.

Recent studies have shown that certain drugs can produce experiences that can resemble NDEs. While certain elements could be similar to actual NDEs, lucid dreams and chemical reactions cannot explain how people see certain objects and events outside of the body. Furthermore, they cannot explain how blind people have visual experiences or how people meet relatives that they never knew.

## NDEs Provide False Hope, As Unbelievers Have Experienced Heaven

It is true that from time-to-time atheists report their encounters of heaven. But it must be remembered that the person did not remain dead. God desires to see all souls saved. For such individuals, their brief encounter with heaven may have been God's apologetic to bring them to faith. Dr. Barry Levinthal told about the visions that many victims of the Nazi concentration camps had of Jesus. They called him the "Mystery Messiah." Others who were formerly part of ISIS have had visions of Jesus and became disciples of Christ all because of their experiences. God's apologetic evangelism is far greater than anything we could ever offer. Don't be surprised if God uses revolutionary ways to reach the most inaccessible people.

## NDEs are Unbiblical

We already provided a case to show how NDEs can fit within a biblical paradigm. If one ascribes to soul survival in the intermediate state and accepts the biblical teachings of one being instantly in the presence of God after death, then NDEs hold no problem with orthodox Christian teaching. The primary view of the church for two-thousand millennia has been that the soul continues to survive after death.

## NDEs Do Not Hold Any Similarities

A common objection given against NDEs is that the experiences do not hold any similarities. The skeptic would say that given the vast differences between the stories of NDEs, they do not hold any sense of cohesiveness. In stark contrast, Jeffrey Long, MD investigated 1,300 NDE cases from across the world and determined that the cases did indeed hold certain similarities.

1. 75.4% report experiencing an out-of-body separation of their consciousness from their bodies.

2. 74.4% report having heightened senses, including experiencing reality that was "more real than the present reality."

3. 76.2% report experiencing incredible emotions and sensations of peace.

4. 33.8% report passing through a tunnel.

5. 64.6 % report seeing a divine being of mystical light.

6. 57.3% report encountering angelic beings, deceased relatives, and/or deceased friends.

7. 60.5% report having an altered sense of space and time.

8. 22.2% experienced a life review.

9. 52.2% report encountering unworldly, heavenly realms.

10. 56% experienced some special learning of life.

11. 31% witnessed some boundary or barrier.

12. 58.5% were aware of their decision to return to the body.[17]

Dr. Long's research has currently grown to over 5,000 NDE reports as of publication and growing exponentially with each passing year. While skeptical at the beginning of his research, Dr. Long now concludes that electrical activity in the lower part of the brain cannot account for the highly lucid and ordered experiences described by NDE accounts. He goes on to say, "Lucidity coupled with the predictable order of [core] elements establishes that NDEs are not dreams or hallucinations, nor are they due to any other causes of impaired brain functioning."[18]

# Safeguards When Evaluating NDEs: ASK

When examining NDEs, it is important to adopt certain safeguards so that we do not thwart our theological perspectives due to subjective testimonies. Because of the nature and grandeur of heaven and the limitation of language, one finds it nearly impossible to completely convey heavenly experiences. Therefore, NDEs are by nature subjective experiences even though they can be proven with objective evidence. We may use the acrostic ASK to help us remember three important traits of NDEs and divine revelation.

## Analogies

Remember that each person will use their own selected analogies to describe eternal sights. People have reported seeing colors that do not exist on this earth, experiencing a sense of timelessness, and feeling pure, unadulterated, expressions of divine love. How do we describe such things in a corporeal, material world? We use analogies from what we know on earth. John and Ezekiel ran into similar issues. That's why apocalyptic literature is full of symbols and metaphorical language.

Dr. Alexander said that he had to use allegories to describe what it was he saw in eternity. How do you describe a place that transcends the material world when what we know most is the material world? How do you describe a timeless place? One must use things they know to describe the things they see. That is why there are differences between NDEs in how things are explained.

17. Burke, *Imagine Heaven*, 46; Long and Perry, *Evidence of the Afterlife*, 6–7.

18. Long and Perry, *Evidence of the Afterlife*, 164.

## Scriptural Priority

When looking into these encounters, remember that God's revelation takes precedence over the stories. If a person claims to have heard something that runs counter to the Scripture, then one must wonder whether the person heard correctly or if he/she is interjecting their philosophy into their experience.

Heaven is beyond space and time. Therefore, it would be difficult for someone to describe. If the modern NDE seems to dispute what is found in the biblical record, it must be remembered that God gave the words to the apostles and prophets to describe heaven. He did not do the same for modern NDEs.

John Burke writes, "These stories are *interpretations* of an experience. The core elements stay amazingly true to Scripture, but we must remain skeptical of outlier details. After reading close to one thousand NDEs, the most common thing I've heard is how impossible it is to put into words. Listen to the struggles that those who had NDE have in trying to explain their experiences:

'There are no human words that even come close.' –Crystal.

'There are no words to express His divine presence.' –Gary.

'What I saw was too beautiful for words.' –Dutch patient.

'The kind of love that I experienced there cannot be expressed in words.' –Suresh."[19]

## Keep Essential Points (Eating Fish analogy)

When it comes to evaluating NDEs, there may be times when believers may want to cast out the objective aspects of a certain NDE due to the subjective elements of the experience due to the person's worldview. In cases such as these, it is best to use the analogy of eating fish. A person eating fish will swallow the meat but spit out the bones. The same is true for all things in life. Find the value in NDEs but spit out anything that does not mesh with the Christian worldview.

19. Long and Perry, *Evidence of the Afterlife*, 51.

# Conclusion

As this chapter has shown, good sound evidence shows that NDEs are real experiences. NDEs provide evidence that the materialist worldview is bankrupt, and that the spiritual realm is very much a reality. But we must understand that NDEs do not trump what is found in Scripture. Scripture must be our ultimate guide when navigating heavenly issues.

To give a personal example on a much smaller frame of reference, I recall my time spent at Liberty University in the Ph.D. program. I attended my on-site graduation in 2016. At that time, my family and I visited the cafeteria, the football field, and Thomas Road Baptist Church. Even though I thought I had seen the entire campus, it was not until I began intensives that I realize how much more there was to the university. My good friend, Dr. Chris Berg, showed me the ropes on how to navigate the massive campus. He guided me to the Freedom Tower and the massive four-story library. If you were to have asked me about the campus in 2016, I would have given you a very limited version of the campus as it exists. The same is true with heaven. The heavenly visitations that we read about with NDE encounters tell us of one person's experience within one small minute sector of a massive heavenly domain. When one considers that we live in a small section of a small planet, orbiting a medium-sized yellow star, centered between two arm bands positioned 2/3 out from the center of one of possibly 200 billion galaxies, arranged in a universe estimated to be 250 times larger than what can be observed;[20] then we can anticipate that heaven will be even bigger. If heaven is larger than the present universe, and God is bigger than both, then no one should ever anticipate that a single individual could see all of heaven in a brief span of time. I believe that we will spend eternity exploring the massive new creation while also forever learning more about God and his being. Heaven is going to be the best possible place that could ever be conceived. NDEs simply reveal the reality of the afterlife. We must be prepared for it. For the believer in Christ, understand that NDEs tell us about the wondrous beauty and love that awaits us. If we could get a taste of heaven, we would never want to come back.

Though I could not see her expression over the phone, the glee in Sandy's voice could not be contained. She was not one given to giddy expressions of emotion. But as I explained the nature of NDEs and the reports

---

20. See Emerging Technology from the ARXiV, "Cosmos at Least 250x Bigger," para. 17, and Tillman and Gordon, "How Big is the Universe," para. 13.

from numerous individuals, she could not contain her joy. Even still, Sandy had one final question that caused a great deal of tension with her perception of heaven. Quite honestly, I dare say that her next question is one that many have thought about but never asked audibly.

# Chapter Nine

# WILL HEAVEN BE BORING?

*Isaiah 65:17–25*

1. Heaven Will Not Be Boring Because of an Exciting New Start (65:17)

2. Heaven Will Not Be Boring Because of an Exciting New Joy (65:18–19)

3. Heaven Will Not Be Boring Because of an Exciting New Health (65:20)

4. Heaven Will Not Be Boring Because of an Exciting New Work (65:21–23)

5. Heaven Will Not Be Boring Because of an Exciting New Adventure (65:24–25)

AT THIS POINT IN our conversation, Sandy became severely concerned. She cleared her throat. Her voice seemed to be a bit shaken. The previous questions had satisfied much of her concern, but she still had one area of concern that highly burdened her. She said, "Pastor, I am going to ask you a question that is going to sound a bit odd. I don't want you to think that I am a heathen or an awful person. I have been afraid to ask a preacher this question because I was afraid that he would say that I am the devil, a heathen, or something." I replied, "Sandy, no matter what question you have, I am sure someone has asked it before." Not knowing what to expect, I continued, "Having been an agnostic at one point in my life, it is highly probable that I asked the same question myself."

Sandy expressed relief, as she no longer seemed shaken. "Well, preacher. Then, I'll come right out and ask it. I like singing just as well as the next person. I have been blessed by the hymns and music played in church. However, I have heard preachers say that all we will do for all eternity is sing, sing, sing. To be frank, I think that will get a bit boring after a while. Sure, if the singing is good, I could go along with it for a while. But if all we do is play harps and sing to our heart's content, that will get awfully boring over time. If this singing goes on and on and on, I'm afraid that I won't enjoy heaven. If that's the case, will God kick me out of heaven for not enjoying an eternal church service? I am afraid that I will be disappointed with heaven." Beginning to sob, she continued, "This is something that keeps me up at night."

Honestly, I had wondered the same thing myself. Sandy was surprised to find that I had asked the same question. Sandy and I are far from being the only ones who have asked this question. In a conversation with my dissertation chair, Dr. Leo Percer, he conveyed that he and some of his students had conversed on the same matter. Church services are great . . . well, let me correct that. *Some* church services are great. With others, one would find more enjoyment in watching paint dry (my words, not Leo Percer's). Yet even with the best of services, it is sometimes difficult to keep people engaged for one hour much less an eternity. Now, I have been told that some of my sermons go on and on. So, how in heaven's name would people survive singing for eternity? (pun intended) Would this perception of heaven not become hellish for some, if not for the majority of people? And if so, would this not hinder heaven from being the place than which nothing greater could be conceived?

Much of this talk of eternal singing comes from two avenues—an exaggeration of the singing explained in Revelation and preachers getting caught up in the moment. The first is self-explanatory as we find numerous passages of Scripture referencing the singing in heaven,[1] but the second will require a brief explanation. Preachers often get caught up

---

1. Two such examples come to mind. Revelation 5:9 says, "And they sang a new song: You are worthy to take the scroll, and to open its seals, because you were slaughtered, and you purchased people for God by your blood from every tribe and language and people and nation." Revelation 14:3 says, "They sang a new song before the throne and before the four living creatures and the elders, but no one could learn the song except the 144,000 who had been redeemed from the earth." Both passages seem to speak of individual instances, not necessarily eternal singing. From what I can find, the only beings that continue to endlessly sing are the four living creatures around God's throne (Rev. 4:8).

in the moment and say things that they have not thought through. This is perhaps one such example.

I told Sandy that I thought that heaven would be an exciting place as it is full of activities that complement different people. It is important to note that God created us all as different individuals for a reason. We all have different likes and dislikes, all with different personalities. Heaven will be enjoyable for all who inherit it. For those of us who enjoy a good intellectual dialogue, we will find that in heaven. For those who enjoy games, I think they will be found there, as well. For those like myself who enjoy times of contemplative solitude and with small groups, heaven will have times for people like us. For those who enjoy being in the company of mass numbers of people, there will be times for extroverts, as well.

Randy Alcorn argues that the claim that heaven is boring stems from a misunderstanding of God's character. Alcorn asserts, "Our belief that Heaven will be boring betrays a heresy—that God is boring. There's no greater nonsense."[2] While I would not go so far as to equate the belief as a heresy, Alcorn is correct in the sense that our perceptions of heaven as boring largely ignore the exciting presence of the Creator. But perhaps this is also true for those who equivocate heaven in a one-dimensional manner. Heaven is much greater than we realize because God is greater than all.

As the premise of this book has noted, if God is that than which nothing greater can be conceived and heaven is God's greatest gift to humanity, then heaven is that place than which nothing greater could be conceived. If heaven is simply eternal singing with nothing more, then that will not minister to the needs of all its inhabitants, therefore leaving it less than ideal and less than the greatest place that could be conceived. Now, if your ideal is singing for eternity, I am sure there will be opportunities for you to do so. But for others who do not see that as equally enjoyable, they will not be coerced to participate against their will.

Heaven will be so enjoyable that it reminds me of a story I heard about an 85-year-old couple who died in a car accident after having been married for sixty years. They had been in good health for the last ten years mainly due to the wife's interest in health food and exercise. When they reached the pearly gates, their guide led them to a mansion decked out with a beautiful kitchen, a master suite, and equipped with a Jacuzzi. They were amazed by all the grandeur before their eyes. The old man, who was known as a tight-wad, asked their angelic guide, "Just how much is all this going to cost?"

2. Alcorn, *Heaven*.

The angel, "Sir, this is all free. This is heaven. It comes equipped with all kinds of luxuries including a championship golf course which is adjacent to your mansion."

The old man asked, "How much are the green fees?" The angel noted again, "Sir, this is heaven. There's no charge." "Well how about the buffet? Surely there's a charge to eat all that food." The angel again responded, "Sir, this is heaven. It's all free. You can eat all you want, as much as you want, and you'll never gain weight." "But sir, where are the low-cholesterol foods?" The angel replied, "There's no need to worry about cholesterol. We have no cholesterol problems in heaven."

Surprising to all, the man became enraged. The angel and the man's wife were surprised. The wife asked, "Honey, this place is perfect! Why are you so angry?" The man charged, "Angry? Yes, I am angry! If it weren't for your blasted bran muffins, we could have been here ten years ago!"

Heaven is going to be an exciting place for everyone who enters. It won't be a place that tortures people who are non-music lovers with continuous singing. Rather, heaven is a lively, exciting place that has something that everyone will enjoy. The reason I emphasize the singing part is due to Sandy's reservations about eternal singing. But there may be other areas that preachers have promoted about heaven that do not necessarily sit well with all believers. In Isaiah 65, the prophet paints a picture of heaven that is very different than the one portrayed by one-dimensional thinking that has plagued the minds of many heaven-seekers. Heaven will not be boring because it features an exciting new start, newfound joy, amazing health, enjoyable work, and exciting adventures.

## Heaven Will Not Be Boring Because of an Exciting New Start (65:17)

As he does in Revelation, God promises that he will create a "new heaven and a new earth" (65:17). God will grant a new start to creation itself. As was previously mentioned, the laws of physics will be vastly different in the new creation as they currently exist. Because of this new creation, it is important to also note that the new creation provides a new start. Isaiah 65 states that "past events will not be remembered or come to mind" (65:17). Everyone will get a new start. Let us look at these two themes a bit deeper.

First, in heaven, creation itself will get a new jumpstart. In many ways, creation will return to the paradise of the Garden of Eden before the entrance of sin into the world.[3] Can you imagine a time when the weather is not extremely hot or extremely cold? Can you imagine a time when mosquitoes will not pester you? Creation itself will be harmonious. This is what heaven will be like. Nothing is boring about a place of perfection. The tolls of time upon our mortal bodies will not be found in the new creation. Old knees and aching backs will be replaced with bodies that never decay. Oh, how I have longed to return to my powerlifting days in my 30s! As previously mentioned, I was able to hit a great deal of weight in the gym in those days. However, time has wreaked havoc on my knees and back, no longer permitting me to hit the numbers I once did. The new creation will offer the reboot that many of us have so long desired.

Second, individuals will be able to get a new start in life. Many individuals have a past. If someone does something wrong, it is difficult to get a fresh, new start in life, especially if the person lives in a small town. Quite honestly, many people live in shame due to something that happened 50 years ago. Because of their past, they are unable to get the jobs they want or the position in society they desire. Even though some people claim they forgive, they truly don't if they continue to hang a past discretion over the head of the accused.

Think of Mary the mother of Jesus. She did nothing wrong. However, the people in her community shunned her. Later in his ministry, Jesus was called "the son of Mary, and the brother of James, Joses, Judas, and Simon" (Mk. 6:3). It is thought that this expression could have been a slander against Mary and the means by which she gave birth to Jesus.[4] In other words, the people may have called Jesus something comparable to a bastard due to their perception that Mary may have had an adulterous relationship outside of her betrothal to Joseph, which is unfounded. One tradition claims that Mary had been seduced by a Roman soldier named Pandera.[5] But it must be noted that the tradition is plagued with controversy, precluding it from being a real possibility. Nevertheless, if the interpretation holds, then even Mary the mother of Jesus faced scorn and derision that she could never quite shake in the small towns in which she lived.

---

3. Smith, *Isaiah 40–66*, 716.

4. Beare, *Gospel According to Matthew*, 319. For a fuller discussion on the controversy surrounding the text and what may have been in the original, see Edwards, *Gospel According to Mark*, 172; and Brooks, *Mark*, 98–99.

5. *Kohelet Rabbah* 10.5.1.

In stark contrast, a person will be able to truly have a fresh start on life in heaven. Past indiscretions will be forgiven and forgotten. No one will remind them of their past misdeeds or excommunicate them from their social group. In heaven, no one will feel unwanted. No one will feel out of place. Everyone will feel at home. People will truly have the fresh new beginning that they have always craved. A person will live for eternity with nothing from the past hanging over their head. Nothing about that sounds boring.

## Heaven Will Not Be Boring Because Of An Exciting New Joy (65:18–19)

Sandy had mentioned her concern about heaven being boring. After speaking with Sandy, I have been surprised by the number of other people who hold similar concerns. One person even told me, "This is an issue that has bothered me for quite some time." Another person jokingly chided me, saying, "If I make it to heaven, I am hunting you down if heaven turns out to be boring after all." After sharing a laugh, I expressed that I truly believe that heaven will be exciting because it represents one of God's greatest gifts for us. I also promised the person that I would not sing, as I doubt that my singing would sound good even in heaven.

Why am I so confident that heaven will be exciting? As noted, heaven is God's greatest gift to us. Jesus reminds us that "If you then, who are evil, know how to give good gifts to your children, how much more will your Father in heaven give good things to those who ask him" (Matt. 7:11). Thus, if God is that than which nothing greater can be perceived and his gifts are greater than anything we can perceive, then heaven is assuredly more exciting and vibrant than we could ever imagine.

Additionally, Isaiah foretells a heavenly place where people in this new creation would "be glad and rejoice forever" (65:18) because God would create "Jerusalem to be a joy and its people to be a delight" (65:18). Gary Smith noted that the text indicates that the efforts of mankind to evoke this kind of change will be unsuccessful. That is, our work in politics will never bring about this kind of existence. Only the intercessory work of God in creation could arouse such a place.[6] Jerusalem will be a joy to the people of the new creation only because of God's work flowing from the New Jerusalem. One should not take this text to mean that God's work is only in Israel. Rather, his new creation will impact all of creation worldwide,

6. Smith, *Isaiah 40–66*, 718.

with new sights, new sounds, and an incredibly new state of being (see Isa. 41:17–20; 43:16–21; 44:3–5; 48:9–11; 50:1–3).[7]

The point of verse 18 is that people will find exuberant joy in the new creation even though each person is different, and the location is the same. Heaven is going to be a big place with different activities for every person. Everyone holds different preferences about things that bring them enjoyment. For instance, just the other day, my wife and I went to a local Barnes & Noble Bookstore in our area to use a gift card that had been given to me the previous year. I could have spent all day in that beloved place. Perusing the various aisles and the voluminous options was like a little piece of heaven for me. Plus, the arousing aroma of brewing coffee and the smell of freshly printed pages conjure up pleasantries in my mind and soul. Why? I love books and freshly brewed coffee! But the same is not true for my wife. As a non-book lover, a non-coffee drinker, and admittedly suffering from mild OCD, bookstores are problematic for her for two reasons. One, she is not a book lover, as previously noted—a trait that I do not understand as a bibliophile. Two, bookstores bring something out in her OCD as she likes things neat and tidy. Something about bookstores and libraries makes her feel like there is too much clutter. The exact opposite is true when we enter a clothing outlet. She could look at clothes all day long. For me, meh! As long as I have something that fits my expanded frame and is comfortable, I am good. I am ready to leave the clothing store after five minutes of being there. I have even argued with my wife, rather unconvincingly, that clothing outlets are far more cluttered than bookstores and libraries. My only success in this endeavor is to get the classic look. Husbands will understand what I mean here.

The above point merely notes the different preferences we all possess. Could heaven have bookstores and libraries? Certainly. Could heaven have other outlets that my wife would enjoy? Very possibly. Now, one could argue that there will be no money in heaven, and rightfully so. But for the sake of this illustration, humor me for a moment. Because my wife and I have different preferences and enjoyments, heaven will have something for both of us to enjoy. Heaven is not built with only one person in mind. Rather, it is specially designed for all of God's children to enjoy.

Furthermore, God himself will find joy in "Jerusalem and be glad in [his] people" (65:19). Weeping and crying would no longer be found in this new creation (65:19). Not only will people find joy in heaven, but God

7. Smith, *Isaiah 40–66*, 720.

also will find joy in his people. This is a truth that other apocalyptic passages describe. Revelation 22 notes that "God's dwelling is with humanity, and he will live with them. They will be his people, and God himself will be with them and will be their God. He will wipe away every tear from their eyes. Death will be no more; grief, crying, and pain will be no more, because the previous things have passed away" (Rev. 22:3b–4). Heaven is a place where both God and his people are happy. No matter how that looks, it will be good.

I think the reason that many have thought that heaven will be boring is that we connect bad behavior with fun times. Going back to the illustration of the rock band AC/DC's song "Highway to Hell," the songwriters tend to think of hell as a place of fun due to their association of bad behavior with fun times. However, Christians can have a good time together without having to resort to sinful behavior. My wife and I have enjoyed fun times with two godly couples we often meet for supper. We do not get into any mischief. Rather, we enjoy each other's company and have fun together. I also think of a time when my wife and I joined two other couples to see a Christian comedian in concert in Charlotte, North Carolina. A fun time was had by all.

Also, due to common misconceptions about God, people tend to think of God as stiff and wooden. But God seems to have a good sense of humor. Take, for instance, Jesus's parables. Often, Jesus inserted humor and tongue-in-cheek illustrations into his teachings to make a powerful point. The same is true of God's use of the prophets and their prophetic writings.

God proved to have a sense of humor when he called me back into the ministry. The fact that he called a backward, introverted soul like me into public ministry is humorous enough. But when God called me back into the ministry, I told him that I would go anywhere he sent me, as long as the people of that place did not handle snakes.

Would you believe a snake has been found in nearly every place I have served since then? At my first place of ministry, a lady in the church carried a snake out of the church that she had found in the basement. Yes, it can be said that we technically had a snake handler at the Baptist church where God called me after reinstating me. Oh yes, God most definitely has a sense of humor. There is no party or good time that can be had on earth that will come close to matching the great time to be had in heaven. No, we are not going to be playing harps all day. Rather, we will be having fun times with God and with each other.

# Heaven Will Not Be Boring Because of an Exciting New Health (65:20)

This verse can be somewhat confusing because of the language. However, once we decipher the details, we can get a picture of what God is saying through Isaiah about life in the new creation. The first reads, "In her, a nursing infant will no longer live only a few days, or an old man no live out his days. Indeed, the one who dies at a hundred years old will be mourned as a young man, and the one who misses a hundred years will be considered cursed" (Isa. 65:20).

The reader should note that Isaiah is drawing a contrast between the creation that is to the creation that is to come.[8] Isaiah contrasts the old creation with the new creation in three ways. First, Isaiah contrasts infants who die early in the old creation to infants who will never die in the new creation. On the first point, I'm not convinced that there will be different ages of individuals in heaven. I think everyone will be in their prime, at whatever stage that may be. Most have agreed that people reach their full development in their late 20s to early 30s. Perhaps this is the age that people will be in heaven.

Second, Isaiah contrasts a time in the old creation where old men cannot live out their days with the time of the new creation where people will live eternally. On the second point, do not be taken aback by Isaiah's language about people getting old and the cursed one being one who doesn't make it to 100. The reason the one who did not make it to 100 would be considered cursed is that eternal life exists in the new creation.

Third, Isaiah contrasts the early death of individuals in the old creation with the lengthy lifespan of individuals in the new creation, pointing out that those who do not reach 100 years of age would be considered cursed. On the third point, note that we have been separated by death and disease. The issues that plague us in this world will be non-existent in heaven. Can you imagine what it will be like to have a body that never dies?

In a conversation that I had with Dr. Leo Percer, I recall him saying, "If I knew what I know now and had the body that I had in my twenties, I

---

8. Smith, *Isaiah 40–66*, 721. Some also draw a connection to the millennial kingdom. For those redeemed during the time of tribulation, they will not have received a glorified body by that time. See *Moody Bible Commentary*, 1100. While the commentators of the *Moody Bible Commentary* are correct in their assessment, I do not know that it is essential to take that perspective here. Isaiah may only be drawing a contrast between the two spheres of existence.

would be dangerous." I think all of us could say the same. I think back to the body I had in my early twenties and thirties. In powerlifting, I was able to hit numbers that I had difficulties lifting in my forties. My muscles are still capable, but my joints are not able to bear the load.

Millard Erickson suggests that our bodies will be beyond even that of what Jesus held post-resurrection because Jesus underwent a further transformation when he was glorified in heaven.[9] Thus, as Erickson argues, our resurrected bodies will be likened to the glorified resurrection body that Jesus now possesses.[10] Erickson goes on to claim that certain features like eating fish will not be evident in the glorified bodies.[11] It is agreed that our bodies will be likened to the present glorified body of Jesus. But nowhere is it found that food and drinks will not be enjoyed in heaven. Perhaps on this notion, it would be best to remain open to either possibility as we simply do not have enough data to make a clear assessment in either direction. However, I would like to think that we could eat and drink in heaven without the worries of calories.

I say again: Can you imagine what it will be like to have a body that never dies? Can you imagine how nice it will be to never worry about losing children or loved ones? This is the reality of heaven! How could a place like that ever be boring? Rather, it will be incredibly exciting!

## Heaven Will Not Be Boring Because of an Exciting New Work (65:21–24)

Sandy was an extremely hard worker. She worked many years in the textile industry in plants at both Yadkinville and Mocksville, North Carolina. My wife worked with Sandy for many years, and she noted that Sandy always put everything she had into her work. Sandy was anything but lazy. It became difficult for Sandy when she was unable to work and stay active. So, an eternity doing nothing was not something that would appeal to Sandy. Is heaven a place where we merely sit on the front porches of our new heavenly homes doing nothing for all eternity? Absolutely not! Isaiah affords five characteristics of our heavenly home that show the work performed in heaven. However, this work is not something that is done begrudgingly. Rather, this heavenly work fulfills our passions and desires.

9. Erickson, *Christian Theology*, 1100.

10. Erickson, *Christian Theology*, 1100.

11. Erickson, *Christian Theology*, 1100.

First, Isaiah says that in the new creation, "people will build houses and live in them" (65:21). The first point does not necessarily mean that people will have to build homes, but it does not indicate that people will not build things either. On the one hand, Jesus said that he went to heaven to "prepare a place for you . . . If I go away to prepare a place for you, I will come again and take you to myself, so that where I am you may be also" (Jn. 14:2b–3). On the other hand, this does not detract from the possibility that people will build things in heaven, especially those who enjoy working in construction.

The main point being made is that people will not worry about dying before completing their tasks because death no longer exists. How many times have people desired to finish something but were unable to do so because of unforeseen instances? In heaven, people will have the opportunity to live out their dreams that could not be fulfilled on earth. Alcorn notes,

> I believe the New Earth will offer us opportunities we wished for but never had. God's original plan was that human beings would live happy and fulfilling lives on Earth. If our current lives are our only chances at that, God's plan has been thwarted. Consider the injustice—many honest, faithful people never got to live fulfilling lives, while some dishonest and unfaithful people seemed to fare much better.[12]

I also consider the different things I have been unable to do in my life due to certain obligations. I do not begrudge these responsibilities. However, I have not been able to travel or see the many beautiful parts of this world. Others may have desired to get an advanced education but were unable to do so for one reason or another. Heaven will afford its citizens the opportunities that they never had on earth.

Second, Isaiah notes that the people will "plant vineyards and eat their fruit" (65:22). He also states that people would build houses without other people living in them and would not plant vineyards with others eating their fruit (65:22). The prophet's descriptions of building houses without others living in them and planting vineyards without losing them indicate that no crime exists in heaven. You will not have to worry about losing your possessions to others because no one will steal and destroy them. Can you imagine living in a place where doors and windows no longer need to be locked? No one will need 9-1-1 services, no police forces, no fire departments, and no hospitals. Everyone will enjoy the bounty of the things they build and create.

12. Alcorn, *Heaven*.

Third, God says that his chosen ones would "fully enjoy the work of their hands" (65:22). The third point describes the enjoyment that comes from the work of one's hands. When we talk about one's work in heaven, we often think of the 9 to 5 jobs that are currently held, or those from which one retired. Some enjoy the work they do on earth. But the vast majority of people do not. A recent CNBC report noted that a whopping 60 percent of people were unhappy with their jobs.[13] The jobs that we hold in heaven will be things we enjoy doing. These jobs will be linked with our calling and passion. Perhaps these occupations will be jobs we wanted to do, but for whatever reason, we were not able. I do not doubt that there will be classes there for those who want to take them. Can you imagine having Jesus as your teacher teaching about the creation of the world? Or Moses teaching about the mosaic covenant? Or, if that's not your thing, perhaps you could go to the heavenly symphony to hear music that is far greater than you have ever heard. Maybe you could go to Noah's school of ark building. Maybe, if you like strength sports, you could check out Samson's strongman show. Who knows? The point is that the work in heaven will be enjoyable. Our work is and will be a means of worshiping God.

Before I noted how I love bookstores and my wife loves clothing outlets. In like manner, I enjoy teaching and writing books. But for my wife, these things are not enjoyable for her. In contrast, she enjoys home projects and working outdoors. I often find myself getting frustrated with home projects because there is always a board that is not cut right or an outlet that will not install correctly. Here is another example of how two people can find two very different activities enjoyable.

Fourth, the worker is described as one that would be successful in all that one strives to do (65:23). They and their families would be blessed (65:23). The fourth point describes the success we will have in our heavenly pursuits. We will not have to worry about mosquitoes pestering us or anything of the like. If it were possible for us to mess up something in heaven, we have God and several others who would help us fix it. We will be successful in our pursuits. Even if there is a chance that we might fail in some capacity in the new creation, it will certainly be possible to quickly fix any mistakes made.

Fifth and finally, God describes the close relationship that he possesses with his people. Before a believer needs anything, God is there to answer.

13. 60 percent were emotionally detached, and 19 percent reported being miserable. Collins, "Job Unhappiness," para. 3.

The final point relates to God's fantastic relationship with us. God is not and will not be a mean, angry taskmaster. Rather, he is a loving Father and friend who is there to give us what we need before we even realize there is a need. Can you imagine if you had an employer who was there to give you extra supplies before you even needed the supplies?

The primary point is this: Heaven only seems boring when we try to put God in a box or limit the activities of heaven. Heaven is far greater than any of us have ever imagined. It will be a bustling, exuberant place full of things to do, people to see, and things to learn and experience. Heaven is not going to be an eternal church service. God's sanctuary is not limited to his throne. Rather, we will worship God in all we do for him in heaven. Additionally, the heavenly citizens will have opportunities with loved ones, activities, and the body that they never had on earth. Before concluding the chapter, consider one last point concerning the bustling activities of heaven.

## Heaven Will Not Be Boring Because of an Exciting New Adventure (65:25)

Isaiah notes that predator and prey will coexist and befriend one another. Evil will be nonexistent in this new creation. Unlike the present time, the "wolf and the lamb will feed together, and the lion will eat straw like cattle" (65:25). The prophet goes on to say that "They will not do what is evil or destroy on my entire holy mountain,' says the Lord" (65:25). With the lack of evil in this new creation, people will be able to explore the new creation in ways that cannot be done in the current creation. Can you imagine all the places we could see with no threat of evil or destruction? For instance, many of the most exotic places on earth cannot be visited due to governmental restrictions, threats to wildlife, or concerns over warring nations and tribes.

In a telephone conversation with Dr. Leo Percer, we discussed the ability to travel to limitless places in the new creation. Dr. Percer's insights resonated with me as I fancy myself an amateur astronomer. On clear night skies, my telescope unveils a kaleidoscopic array of planets, galaxies, and stars that no person will ever be able to visit in our current bodies within the current space-time continuum. Consider this—if one were to travel to Proxima Centauri, our nearest neighboring star outside the solar system, it would take 73,000 years to reach the star while traveling at the rate of

17.3 kilometers a second.[14] If the traveler were to journey at the speed of light—an impossibility with our current bodies—it would still take an estimated 4.22 years to arrive.[15] Additionally, as previously noted, cosmologists estimate that the universe is some 250 times larger than what scientists can observe with their best instruments.[16] With this data in mind, one can deduce that well over 99 percent of the universe will never be explored during this life. The universe is just too big. However, with their new supercharged, glorified, resurrected bodies in eternity, the new creation can be explored without limitations, unlike the present cosmos.

## Conclusion

After describing the thrilling things awaiting us in heaven and in the new creation to come, Sandy was more excited and at ease about the heavenly home awaiting her after our conversation. She even noted that she had never heard heaven described in the manner that we discussed. This is rather unfortunate, as many people may have had similar doubts about the fun and exciting nature of our heavenly home. A lot of this misconception stems from the way heaven has been presented by expositors of the Word. I often fear that I may have been guilty of doing the same before this heavenly exploration.

Rather than being a one-dimensional place as often portrayed by well-intentioned rhetoricians of the Word, heaven is a multidimensional venue with plenty of excitement for individuals of all tastes and preferences. Perhaps the reason heaven seems boring is that we have limited our understanding of heaven, making it an eternal worship service. While that would still be nice, that doesn't match the reality of what we find in Scripture.

Also as earlier expressed, concerns about heaven being boring greatly misinterprets, or perhaps even distrusts, the loving, benevolent nature of God. As good as the gifts that God gives us on earth, heaven will far exceed anything we can imagine or conceive. As Paul said, "But as it is written, 'What no eye has seen, no ear has heard, and no human heart has conceived—God has prepared these things for those who love him'" (1 Cor. 2:9). If God is the maximally great God that we have presented him to be and heaven is the greatest gift that God has ever given his people, then

14. "Nearest Neighbor Star," para. 3.
15. "Nearest Neighbor Star," para. 3.
16. Tillman and Gordon, "How Big is the Universe?," para. 13.

heaven far exceeds our wildest conceptions as it exists as a place than which nowhere greater could be conceived.

*Chapter Ten*

# CAN I BE SURE THAT I AM GOING TO HEAVEN?

## *1 John 4:16—5:13*

1. The Surety of God's Compassion (4:16–21)

2. The Surety of God's Commandments (5:1–4)

3. The Surety of God's Confirmation (5:5–13)

A FTER SETTLING HER MOST pressing questions, Sandy had one more issue that she needed to work through. Sandy and I had taken a long journey on our two-hour phone call. The pressures she had been carrying for numerous years were now being released. She was as relieved as an individual who just had an infected tooth removed. She was no longer poisoned by her doubts and worries about heaven. She finally found the respite she needed.

However, the conversation was not over just yet. She had one last question that proved to be one of the most emotional, yet the easiest to answer. After a lengthy pause, I asked, "Sandy, are you still there?" "Yes, I am just soaking it all in," she replied. "Is there anything else that I can help you with today?" I inquired. After pausing a few moments, Sandy continued, "Preacher, thank you for taking time with me today. This conversation has been really helpful for me." At this time, the mood of the conversation changed as I could sense relief yet detected one last bit of concern. "I have one more thing that I need to run by you. I haven't always done the right things or said the right things. I am far from a perfect woman. Can I be sure that I am going to heaven?"

I answered with a couple of questions. "Sandy," I queried, "have you received Christ as your Savior?" "Yes, I have." "Do you believe that Jesus is Lord and that God raised him from the dead?" "I sure do," she noted. I then proudly said, "Then, according to Scripture, you are guaranteed a place in heaven." I then quoted Romans 10:9, which states, "If you confess with your mouth, 'Jesus is Lord,' and believe in your heart that God raised him from the dead, you will be saved" (Rom. 10:9). I then quoted Romans 10:13, which notes that "everyone who calls on the name of the Lord will be saved" (Rom. 10:13).

I then said to Sandy, "From the promises of Scripture and the confession of your faith, you can then know that you have a place in heaven when you die." Tears began to flow, and Sandy found the assurance she needed in her salvation. From there, I relayed the information about salvific assurance found in 1 John 4:16—5:13. In this text, the aged apostle John writes about the love of God and the confidence that the believer can find in one's relationship with God. God assures us of salvation because of God's eternal compassion, his commandments, and his ability to conquer sin and evil.

I read a story about an elderly woman who had just returned home from her Wednesday night prayer meeting. As she entered her home, an intruder startled her. As she caught the man in the act of robbery, she yelled, "Stop! Acts 2:38!" Acts 2:38 says that a person should turn from their sin. The burglar stopped dead in his tracks. The woman then calmly called the police and explained what she had done. The police officers cuffed the man to take him to jail. One of the officers asked, "Why did you just stand there? All she did was yell a passage of Scripture at you." "Scripture?!?" replied the burglar. "I thought she said she had an AXE and TWO 38s!"

Can we know that we are going to heaven? Certainly, we need more than an axe and two 38s to get there. Nonetheless, John affords three reasons as to how a person can know whether he or she has a place in heaven when the person dies—the surety of God's compassion (1 Jn. 4:16–21), the surety of God's commandments (1 Jn. 5:1–4), and the surety of God's confirmation (1 Jn. 5:5–13).

## The Surety of God's Compassion (4:16–21)

In 4:16–21, John emphasizes the importance of God's love in three different ways. First, John emphasizes the importance of God's love as a divine attribute. John said that "God is love" (4:16). He does not say that love is God, but rather God is love. Not all love is from God. We love many things. Some of the things we love are not great and are not good for us. For instance, addicts love those things to which they are addicted. For those addicted to alcohol, their desire will be for their next drink. Those addicted to drugs yearn for the next hit of their drug of choice. Some people are drawn to the bad boy or bad girl and desire the perceived excitement they bring. However, all those forms of love are flawed. Rather, John says that God is love. Love is a pivotal attribute of God.

The late theologian Thomas Oden writes, "That God is love implies that benevolent affection, good will, and empathic understanding are the characteristic qualities in God through which God relates compassionately to creatures."[1] Love is a fundamental attribute of God and critical in understanding why God would desire to save humanity.[2] God's love is relational as, in the words of Adam Harwood, "God acted out of concern for the welfare of people he created and loves, though they are sinners and his enemies."[3] This love is relationally poured out into the lives of God's people through the Holy Spirit. Augustine of Hippo contends that the Holy Spirit is God's bond of love with us and connects us to his divine grace.[4] Thus, God teaches us the true nature of love, and God's influence will lead individuals to love others because of his great love for them.

Second, John notes that God's love leads the believer to a knowledge of God and belief in him. Because God loves us, God has revealed himself to us. If God did not care about us, he would not have concerned himself with

1. Oden, *Living God*, 118.

2. This is a concept that is also asserted by Stanley Grenz. See Grenz, *Theology and the Community of God*, 72.

3. Harwood, *Christian Theology*, 182.

4. "Wherefore also the Holy Spirit consists in the same unity of substance, and in the same equality. For whether He is the unity of both, or the holiness, or the love, or therefore the unity because the love, and therefore the love because the holiness, it is manifest that He is not one of the two, through whom the two are joined, through whom the Begotten is loved by the Begetter, and loves Him that begat Him, and through whom, not by participation, but by their own essence, neither by the gift of any superior, but by their own, they are "keeping the unity of the Spirit in the bond of peace." Augustine of Hippo, *On the Trinity* 6.5, 100.

revealing himself and would have let us devour ourselves. But, because of his love, he has taught us about himself. God's connection with us through the Holy Spirit is one such way God reveals himself to the world. Through Christ, God revealed his sacrificial love for others as he initiated reconciliation with sinners through the atonement of Christ on the cross.[5]

Third, John describes the transformation that happens within a person once he or she experiences God's love. A person's love is made complete when one experiences the love of God. The person will know what love is about. In love, there is no fear (4:18). When a person receives perfect love, the person will want to share that kind of love with others. That is why John strongly asserts that a person cannot say that he or she loves God while living in a state of hatred toward others. John calls the person who claims to love God and hates others a liar (4:20). Strong language but to the point.

Over my 20-plus years of ministry, I have had the opportunity to officiate many weddings. I have advised many couples to look to God if they want to know about true love. Because God is love, he is the source of love. And if God is the source of love, then his love is unadulterated and is not obfuscated by the sinful and often confusing desires of the flesh. Often, human desires are self-centered, myopic, delusional, and driven by one's innate passions. However, God's love is pure, holy, authentic, and sacrificial. God's love is made by choice and driven by what is best for the beloved. Imagine having relationships like that in life. Perhaps the reason that so many marriages end in divorce is that human love is driven by human passions rather than the example of divine love.

I think that the reason we often doubt our salvation is that we still are caught up in a work-based mindset. We understand how unworthy we are. We understand that we fail. Because of that, we feel that we do not deserve heaven. The truth is, we are right on all points. But the point of the gospel is that God has given us heaven. None of us deserve heaven. Rather, God's grace won! As Paul reminds us, "For you are saved by grace through faith, and this is not from yourselves; it is God's gift—not from works, so that no one can boast" (Eph. 2:8–9).

## The Surety of God's Commandments (5:1–4)

Second, the apostle John describes God's commandments, particularly emphasizing our need for obedience. Considering the enormous amount

---

5. Harwood, *Christian Theology*, 182.

of debt the believer owes to God, each child of God should desire to obey the commandments of God. His commandments are not burdensome. The believer should be led to obey God's commandments out of a heart of thanksgiving. John mentions a couple of important truths related to God's commandments. When one discusses God's commandments, one describes the orders given by God to his people.

The first important position John describes is that God's commands are not burdensome (5:3) because God will always fulfill his promises. Scripture notes that God is trustworthy because of two reasons: one, God is unchanging, and two, God cannot lie. God is unchanging, which means that his attributes do not change. The prophet Malachi teaches this concept, saying, "Because I, the Lord, have not changed, you descendants of Jacob have not been destroyed" (Mal. 3:6). James notes that "Every good and perfect gift is from above, coming down from the Father of lights, who does not change like shifting shadows" (Jms. 1:17). The writer of Hebrews reminds that Jesus himself does not change either as he is the "same yesterday, today, and forever" (Heb. 13:8).

Furthermore, God cannot tell a lie. Paul, writing to Titus, says "in the hope of eternal life that God, who cannot lie, promised before the world began" (Tit. 1:2). Moses adds that "God is not a man, that he might lie, or a son of man, that he might change his mind. Does he speak and not act, or promise and not fulfill?" (Num. 23:19). So, if God cannot lie and is unchanging, then God will fulfill all the promises that he has made which remove any concern that God will recant. Thus, a believer should live in obedience to the Lord without having to constantly worry about doing something that will forfeit his or her relational status with God.

Second, John contends that a person who loves God will desire to serve him, not out of obligation, but out of desire (5:1–3). When a person receives the salvation of God, he or she should realize how indebted one is to God. A person will desire to show God's love to others because of the indebtedness one feels to the overwhelming love that God has extended to them. Obedience should not be a matter of obligation, but rather a matter of inclination.

John may have had in mind one of Jesus's teachings where he said, "I give you a new command: Love one another. Just as I have loved you, you are also to love one another. By this everyone will know that you are my disciples, if you love one another" (Jn. 13:34–35). If we are known by the love we have for each other, are people able to denote God's love in our lives simply by our behavior? Would we have evidence of Christ's love in our lives?

Admittedly, and trying my best not to sound judgmental, the modern apologetic community could learn a lot from John's teaching on heavenly obedience and love. In my observations, it seems as if many modern defenders are inclined to snarkiness, mockery, and derision in their interactions with others. It does not end with Christian defenders. Recently, a waitress informed us that the restaurant she worked for recently decided to close on Sundays. One may be inclined to think that the restaurant owners decided to allow their employees off to worship on Sundays. However, they chose to close their doors on Sundays due to the nasty behavior of their church-going patrons. Consider the irony. Church-going Christians hear about the love and grace of God in their churches, only to enter a restaurant after their services to act ungraciously and unlovingly. There is no wonder that the number of churchgoers is drastically declining with this kind of Christian behavior.

## The Surety of God's Confirmation (5:5–13)

Third and finally, John describes the assurance we have in our salvation by God's conquering of sin and death because of several confirmations that God has established: the work of Jesus in his atonement (blood), the work of the Holy Spirit (Spirit), and the testimony (baptism). The aged apostle avers that the "Spirit, the water, and the blood" (1 Jn. 5:7) describe the three confirmations, or testimonies, of God's victory over sin.

### The Confirmation of Blood: The Work of Jesus Fulfilling the New Covenant

The blood refers to Jesus's atoning death. In verse 6, Jesus is shown to have come by water and blood, noting the baptism of Jesus (the beginning of his ministry) and the completion found in his atoning death. God's atoning work is essential in a person's salvation (5:10). The atoning work of Christ on the cross fulfilled the necessary requirements to establish the new covenant. When we receive the work of Christ in our lives, we enter into this new covenantal agreement that God has established with humanity. The person identifies with Christ's completed work on the cross.

## The Confirmation of the Holy Spirit

The Spirit is identified as One who confirms the testimony of a person's salvation. The Spirit testifies and is identified with the truthfulness of God since the Holy Spirit is God (5:5). Scripture provides ample reasons for believing that the Holy Spirit is God. The Holy Spirit bears all the divine attributes of the Father. For instance, the Holy Spirit is omnipotent (Lk. 1:35; Rom. 15:19), omniscient (Jn. 16:13; 1 Cor. 2:10–11), eternal (Heb. 1:10–12; Rev. 1:4; 4:5), and omnipresent (Psa. 139). The Holy Spirit is also linked with the *Shekinah Glory* in the OT (Exod. 25:8; 29:45; and Ezek. 43:1–12). Therefore, if the Holy Spirit is God and the Holy Spirit is in a person's life, that means that God has received that person into a covenant relationship. Paul teaches that the Holy Spirit is the seal of our redemption (Eph. 1:13). If the Holy Spirit is in a person's life, then the person has God's confirmation that he or she is saved.

## The Confirmation of Our Identification with Christ Through Our Baptism

John also draws a connection with the believer's baptism. Baptism does not save us, but it does associate us with Christ's baptism and the community of faith. Baptism publicly acknowledges our entrance into the new covenant through Christ's atoning work on the cross and the infilling of the Holy Spirit. As many pastors have noted, baptism is the outward manifestation of an inward transformation. Because of the confirmation we have in Christ through our baptism, we have a great assurance that we are saved. That is why John says, "I have written these things to you who believe in the name of the Son of God so that you may know that you have eternal life" (5:13).

In many ways, the believer can have better assurance in one's salvation than even a confirmation from an Air BnB. Often, while taking the intensives at Liberty University for my Ph.D., I stayed in an Air BnB. Before traveling the two-and-a-half hours up to Lynchburg, Virginia from Pilot Mountain, North Carolina, I double-checked my itinerary to ensure that I had confirmation from the Air BnB owner. The confirmation ensured that the house was ready for my stay. Good owners would send both a confirmation and a welcome message that noted where to find the necessary toiletries and other items. In like manner, the presence of the Holy Spirit, the association with Christ's atoning work, and baptism in our lives all serve as

God's confirmation that heaven is confirmed. Everything has been set up, and our heavenly, eternal home awaits us when we arrive.

Believers do not have to continuously wonder whether they are saved or not. This can lead to insanity as it nearly did for John Bunyan, the author of *Pilgrim's Progress*, and Martin Luther. We can know with great certainty whether we are saved. If we are saved, then we know that we have a place in heaven, and no one or nothing can ever separate us from the assurance we have of God's unending love (Rom. 8:31–39). Rather than living in worry, believers can rest with great assurance, thereby allowing them to live their fullest lives for Christ while on earth.

## Conclusion

There is a story of a young man who had been raised as an atheist and was training to be an Olympic diver. An outspoken Christian friend was the only religious influence in his life. Because of his friend's outspoken and gregarious nature, the young man heard his friend's messages but never paid much attention to them.

One night, the diver went to the indoor pool at the college he attended. The lights were off, but as the pool had big skylights and the moon was bright, there was plenty of light by which he could see how to get into the pool to practice. The young man climbed up to the highest diving board and as he turned his back to the pool on the edge of the diving board and extended out his arms, he saw the shadow of his body in the shape of a cross. The man became convicted at that moment and realized his need for salvation. So, he knelt and asked Christ to come into his life.

As the young man stood with new life and vigor, the pool's maintenance man walked in and turned on the lights. He yelled for the young man not to dive because the pool had been drained for repairs. The young man was saved both physically and spiritually from a horrible fate that night.

Christians have the assurance of their salvation through God's compassion, commandments, and confirmation. If you have placed your faith in Christ, trust him to do what he has promised to do. Realize that salvation is God's gift to you. You did not earn it yourself. Finally, realize that your work for Christ matters. God did not save you to leave you as you are. He saved you to transform you into his image.

As I explained the assurance believers have in Christ, the last vestige of Sandy's skepticism peeled away, leaving her with the loving confidence that she had a place in heaven. Though I could not see Sandy's face, I detected that she may have had a few tears flow down her cheeks as the sound of her voice had completely changed. With no other questions remaining, Sandy thanked me numerous times for spending the two hours we shared over the phone. Ironically, after our telephone call, the clouds that had caused the overcast sky parted, allowing the rays of sunshine to illuminate the sanctuary once again through the colorful stained-glass windows. The light of the sanctuary metaphorically resembled the light of hope that God gave Sandy that day.

I am not sure if I accomplished much after Sandy and I finished our conversations about heaven that day. As I recall, I think I may have taken a lunch break at a local café to give me time to reflect on the telephone call. Quite honestly, our conversation still resonates with me to this day because of the numerous questions she left with me. How was it that she felt that she had no place in heaven? Why was she led to believe that heaven was boring? Most importantly, how many others may be left with these feelings due to some hurt experienced at church or with church leaders?

My prayer is that my conversations with Sandy will help you as you have your own conversations about heaven. By doing so, my prayer is that you will realize that since God is that than which nothing greater could be conceived, and that heaven will be a place than which nowhere greater could be conceived, then heaven will be far greater than you or I could ever imagine.

# EPILOGUE

U NBEKNOWNST TO ME AT the time, Sandy was battling a terminal illness. A few months after we spoke, I was called to another church in the Pilot Mountain region. Around six to eight months after our conversation, I received word that Sandy had passed away on Wednesday, June 5, 2019. I was deeply honored when her family asked me to officiate her funeral. They told me that her wish was for me to preach at her funeral because of the great comfort that our conversations brought her. Before her funeral, I was told by her family and friends that she was filled with hope and no longer feared death. She faced death with a newfound excitement that she had not previously held. Sandy was excited to go to heaven because she realized that she would be welcomed and accepted. Second to baptizing my son, my encounter with Sandy and the encouragement that God allowed me to provide her was by far one of my proudest moments in ministry.

Her funeral was held on Thursday, June 13, 2019, at the chapel of the local funeral home. I recalled the conversations we shared and my wonderful experiences with Sandy. After the service, the funeral procession led us to a graveside service at the Boyer's Chapel Church of Christ Cemetery. For a Thursday in early June, it was an unusually windy day. The funeral director had me stand at the head of the casket just outside the visitation tent. As I delivered the final words of her committal, a bouquet of flowers fell onto my leg. I stood the flowers back up before continuing with the service. A few statements more and the bouquet fell on my leg once more. I reached down to set the flowers back in their place. As I started to pray, the bouquet fell on my leg yet again. This time, the funeral director staked the flowers into the ground. After I finished praying, the flowers fell over once more.

The director once again staked them in place even saying under his breath, "What is up with these flowers?"

I walked over to shake hands with each family member and offered my condolences. Once I stood back in place to allow the funeral director time to finish up with the family, I looked down to see that the flowers had again fallen onto my leg. This time, I reached down and picked up the flowers, only to notice a large picture of Sandy, sporting a large, mischievous grin. It was the same picture of Sandy that is posted on the Acknowledgements page of this book.

In her own way, Sandy thanked me for our conversations beyond the grave, as she now experienced the glorious splendor of her heavenly home. She had no more pain, no more disease, and no more fears. Now, only love, joy, peace, and goodness would be what she experienced for all eternity. Ironically, after I noticed her picture and set the flowers back in place, they never fell again. You can call it a coincidence. But in my heart, I know that Sandy was reaching out to me in her unique manner.

Since then, I have worked as a hospice chaplain and continued to serve as a pastor in various locales. From firsthand observation, people face their mortality with greater confidence if they have a sense of hope. Nothing can offer eternal hope like the promises of our sovereign God and Jesus his Messiah. Your relationship with God is the most important relationship that can be had because God is the One who will escort you into eternity and into the eternal home that he has created for you. In heaven, you will be welcomed. You will be loved. You will be home.

Church tradition states that theologian Thomas Aquinas laid aside his pen on December 6th, 1273. Aquinas had a vision of heaven that impacted him so deeply that he was unable to continue writing his *Summa Theologica*. Though he had written thousands of pages and committed himself to deep philosophical and theological scholarship, Aquinas quipped, "I can do no more. The end of my labors has come. Such things have been revealed to me that all that I have written seems to me as so much straw."[1] He is then reported to have said, "The most perfect union with God is the most perfect human happiness and the goal of the whole of the human life, a gift that must be given to us by God."[2] Aquinas died just three months after his vision.

---

1. Ryan, "Why Aquinas Didn't Finish," para. 9.
2. Ryan, "Why Aquinas Didn't Finish," para. 10.

Some may read through this book and assert that some of these claims are mere speculation. In some instances, that could prove true. Nonetheless, if God is God, then he must be a maximally great Being who is far greater than anything anyone could ever conceive. If heaven is the greatest place that a maximally great Being could offer, then it is not outside the possibility that our speculations could prove to be true, especially in areas where they intersect the revealed Word of God. Even the best speculations that any of us could muster will be proven to be insufficient when compared to the magnificent heavenly reality that lies ahead. It may be said, like Aquinas, that our best efforts to understand heaven are but straw compared to the wondrous glories lying ahead. If so, our greatest adventure, our greatest hope, and our greatest existence lie beyond the scope of this mortal world. Heaven will be far greater than you ever imagined because it is the greatest place that could ever be conceived.

# BIBLIOGRAPHY

Achtemeier, Paul J., ed. *Harper's Bible Dictionary*. San Francisco: Harper & Row, 1985.

Alcorn, Randy. *Heaven*. Carol Stream, IL: Tyndale Momentum, 2011. Logos Bible Software.

Alexander, Eben. *Proof of Heaven: A Neurosurgeon's Journey into the Afterlife*. New York: Simon & Schuster, 2012.

Anselm. *Proslogium; Monologium; An Appendix, In Behalf of the Fool, by Gaunilon; and Cur Deus Homo*. Translated by Sidney Norton Deane. Chicago: The Open Court Publishing Company, 1939.

Aquinas, Thomas. *A Summa of the Summa*. Edited by Peter Kreeft. San Francisco, CA: Ignatius, 1990.

———. *Summa Theologica*. Translated by the Fathers of the English Dominican Province. London: Burns, Oates & Washbourne, 1921. Logos Bible Software.

Athanasius, *Incarnation of the Word*. Translated by T. Herbert Bindley. London, UK: Religious Tract Society, 1903.

Augustine of Hippo. *On the Trinity*. In *St. Augustine: On the Holy Trinity, Doctrinal Treatises, Moral Treatises*. A Select Library of the Nicene and Post-Nicene Fathers of the Christian Church, First Series. Volume Three. Edited by Philip Schaff. Translated by Arthur West Haddan. Buffalo, NY: Christian Literature Company, 1887.

*b. Hagigah* 16a, https://www.sefaria.org/Chagigah.16a.8?lang=bi.

Baggett, David, and Jerry L. Walls. *Good God: The Theistic Foundations of Morality*. Oxford, UK: Oxford University Press, 2011.

Barker, Kenneth L., and John R. Kohlenberger, III. *Expositor's Bible Commentary: Old Testament*. Abridged edition. Grand Rapids, MI: Zondervan, 2004.

Barry, John D., ed. *Lexham Bible Dictionary*. Bellingham, WA: Lexham, 2016.

Beale, G. K. *Book of Revelation: A Commentary on the Greek Text*. Grand Rapids, MI: Eerdmans, 1999.

Beare, Francis Wright. *The Gospel According to Matthew: A Commentary*. New York: Harper & Row, 1982.

Blau, Ludwig, and Kaufmann Kohler. "Angelology." *JewishEncyclopedia.com* (1906). http://www.jewishencyclopedia.com/articles/1521-angelology#anchor20.

Blomberg, Craig L. *Matthew.* New American Commentary 22. Edited by David S. Dockery. Nashville, TN: B&H, 1992.

Boxall, Ian. *The Revelation of Saint John.* London, UK: Continuum, 2006.

Brooks, James A. *Mark.* New American Commentary 23. Edited by David S. Dockery. Nashville, TN: B&H, 1992.

Brunner, Emil. *The Christian Doctrine of the Church, Faith, and the Consummation.* Philadelphia: Westminster, 1962.

Burke, John. *Imagine Heaven: Near-Death Experiences, God's Promises, and the Exhilarating Future That Awaits You.* Grand Rapids, MI: Baker, 2015.

Ciampa, Roy E., and Brian S. Rosner. *The First Letter to the Corinthians.* The Pillar New Testament Commentary. Grand Rapids, MI: Eerdmans, 2010.

Collins, Leah. "Job Unhappiness is at a Staggering All-Time High According to Gallup." *CNBC.com*, August 12, 2022. https://www.cnbc.com/2022/08/12/job-unhappiness-is-at-a-staggering-all-time-high-according-to-gallup.html.

Davies, W. D. *Paul and Rabbinic Judaism: Some Rabbinic Elements in Pauline Theology.* London: SPCK, 1970.

Davis, John J. *Moses and the Gods: Studies in Exodus.* Winona Lake, IN: BMH, 1986.

Easley, Kendell H. *Revelation.* Holman New Testament Commentary 12. Nashville, TN: Broadman & Holman, 1998.

Edwards, James R. *Gospel According to Mark.* Pillar New Testament Commentary. Grand Rapids, MI: Eerdmans, 2002.

Elwell, Walter A., ed. *Evangelical Commentary on the Bible.* Grand Rapids, MI: Baker, 1995.

Emerging Technology from the ARXiV. "Cosmos at Least 250x Bigger than Visible Universe Say Cosmologists." *TechnologyReview.com*, February 1, 2011. https://www.technologyreview.com/2011/02/01/197279/cosmos-at-least-250x-bigger-than-visible-universe-say-cosmologists/.

Erickson, Millard J. *Christian Theology.* 3rd ed. Grand Rapids: Baker Academic, 2013.

———. *God the Father Almighty: A Contemporary Exploration of the Divine Attributes.* Grand Rapids, MI: Baker, 1998.

Eusebius of Caesarea. *Church History.* In *Eusebius: Church History, Life of Constantine the Great, and Oration in Praise of Constantine.* A Select Library of the Nicene and Post-Nicene Fathers of the Christian Church, Second Series. Volume One. Edited by Philip Schaff and Henry Wace. Translated by Arthur Cushman McGiffert. New York: Christian Literature Company, 1890.

Evans, Tony. *Tony Evans' Book of Illustrations.* Chicago: Moody Press, 2009.

Frankel, Ellen, and Betty Teutsch. *The Encyclopedia of Jewish Symbols.* Lanham, MD: Rowman & Littlefield, 1992.

Freedman, David Noel, et al., eds. *Eerdmans Dictionary of the Bible.* Grand Rapids, MI: Eerdmans, 2000.

Garland, David E. *2 Corinthians.* The New American Commentary 29. Nashville: B&H, 1999.

Geisler, Norman L. *Systematic Theology: In One Volume.* Minneapolis, MN: Bethany, 2011.

Gentry, Thomas J., II. *Absent from the Body, Present with the Lord: Biblical, Theological, and Rational Arguments against Purgatory.* Eugene, OR: Wipf & Stock, 2019.

Grenz, Stanley J. *Theology and the Community of God.* Grand Rapids, MI: Eerdmans, 1994.

Grudem, Wayne. *Systematic Theology: An Introduction to Biblical Doctrine.* 2nd ed. Grand Rapids, MI: Zondervan Academic, 2020.

Hanhart, K. *The Intermediate State*. Groningen, NL: V. R. B. Kleine, 1966.

Harwood, Adam. *Christian Theology: Biblical, Historical, and Systematic*. Bellingham, WA: Lexham, 2022.

Hastings, James, ed. *Encyclopedia of Religion and Ethics*. New York: Scribner, 1955.

Heiser, Michael S. *The Unseen Realm: Recovering the Supernatural Worldview of the Bible*. Bellingham, WA: Lexham, 2015.

Hodge, Charles. *An Exposition of the Second Epistle to the Corinthians*. New York: Robert Carter & Brothers, 1857.

Hodgin, Michael. *1001 Humorous Illustrations for Public Speaking*. Grand Rapids: Zondervan, 1994.

Jeffress, Robert. "Principles to Evaluate Near-Death Experiences." *ptv.org*, October 3, 2019. https://ptv.org/devotional/principles-to-evaluate-near-death-experiences/.

Keener, Craig S. *Revelation*. NIV Application Commentary. Grand Rapids, MI: Zondervan, 2000.

———. *The Gospel of Matthew: A Socio-Rhetorical Commentary*. Cambridge, UK: Eerdmans, 2009.

Kurtz, Paul. *Toward a New Enlightenment: The Philosophy of Paul Kurtz*. Piscataway, NJ: Transaction, 1991.

Lea, Thomas D. *Hebrews, James*. Holman New Testament Commentary. Volume Ten. Nashville, TN: B&H, 1999.

Lenski, R. C. H. *The Interpretation of St. John's Revelation*. Columbus, OH: Lutheran Book Concern, 1935.

Long, Jeffrey, and Paul Perry. *Evidence of the Afterlife: The Science of Near-Death Experiences*. New York: HarperOne, 2011.

Louw, Johannes P., and Eugene Albert Nida. *Greek-English Lexicon of the New Testament: Based on Semantic Domains*. New York: United Bible Societies, 1996.

MacMullen, Ramsay. *Christianizing the Roman Empire, A.D. 100–400*. New Haven, CT: Yale University Press, 1984.

Mangun, Douglas, ed. *Lexham Theological Wordbook*. Bellingham, WA: Lexham, 2014.

Martin, D. B. *The Corinthian Body*. New Haven, CT: Yale University Press, 1999.

Moody, Raymond. Lecture, Lousiana State University (April 26, 1987).

Morse, Melvin, and Paul Perry. *Closer to the Light: Learning from the Near-Death Experiences of Children*. New York: Random House/Villard, 1990.

"The Nearest Neighbor Star." *NASA.gov*, https://imagine.gsfc.nasa.gov/features/cosmic/nearest_star_info.html.

*Numbers Rabbah* 14:3; *Hullin* 89a.

Oden, Thomas C. *The Living God: Systematic Theology*. Volume One. San Francisco, CA: HarperSanFrancisco, 1992.

———. *The Word of Life: Systematic Theology*. Volume Two. San Francisco, CA: HarperSanFrancisco, 1992.

———. *Classic Christianity*. New York: HarperOne, 1992.

Packer, J. I. *Concise Theology: A Guide to Historic Christian Beliefs*. Wheaton, IL: Tyndale House, 1993.

Pohle, Joseph. *The Catholic Doctrine of the Last Things: A Dogmatic Treatise*. St. Louis: B. Herder, 1917.

Ring, Kenneth, and Sharon Cooper. *Mindsight: Near-Death and Out-of-Body Experiences in the Blind*. Bloomington, IN: iUniverse, 2008.

Robinson, J. A. T. *The Body*. SBT 1. London: A. R. Allenson, 1952.

Rogers, John H. *The Giant Planet Jupiter.* Cambridge, UK: Cambridge University Press, 1995.

Ross, Hugh. *Hidden Treasures in the Book of Job: How the Oldest Book in the Bible Answers Today's Scientific Questions.* Grand Rapids, MI: Baker, 2011.

Ryan, George. "Why Aquinas Didn't Finish His Summa . . ." *uCatholic.com*, February 5, 2019. https://ucatholic.com/blog/why-aquinas-didnt-finish-his-summa-a-vision-of-heaven-made-the-prolific-writer-put-down-his-pen/. Accessed December 4, 2022.

Rydelnik, Michael, and Michael Vanlaningham, eds. *Moody Bible Commentary.* Chicago: Moody, 2014.

Seifrid, Mark A. *The Second Letter to the Corinthians.* Pillar New Testament Commentary. Edited by D. A. Carson. Grand Rapids, MI: Eerdmans, 2014.

*Seventh-Day Adventists Answer Questions on Doctrine.* Washington: Review & Herald, 1957.

Smith, Gary V. *Isaiah 40–66.* New American Commentary 15B. Edited by E. Ray Clendenen. Nashville, TN: B&H, 2009.

Strong, James. *Enhanced Strong's Lexicon.* Bellingham, WA: Logos Bible Software, 1995.

Swanson, James. *Dictionary of Biblical Languages with Semitic Domains.* Bellingham, WA: Logos Bible Software, 1997.

"The Nearest Neighbor Star." *NASA.gov.* https://imagine.gsfc.nasa.gov/features/cosmic/nearest_star_info.html. Accessed December 4, 2022.

Thiselton, Anthony C. *Systematic Theology.* Grand Rapids, MI: Eerdmans, 2015.

Tillmann, Nola Taylor, and Jonathan Gordon. "How Big is the Universe?" *Space.com*, January 28, 2022. https://www.space.com/24073-how-big-is-the-universe.html.

Walter A. Elwell, ed. *Evangelical Commentary on the Bible.* Baker Reference Library. Grand Rapids, MI: Baker, 1995.

Walvoord, J. F., and Roy B. Zuck, eds. *The Bible Knowledge Commentary: An Exposition of the Scriptures.* Wheaton, IL: Victor, 1985.

Wright, N. T. *The Resurrection of the Son of God.* Minneapolis, MN: Fortress, 2003.

# INDEX

# Index

# INDEX